Athlone French Poets

PAUL VERLAINE
Romances sans Paroles

Athlone French Poets

General Editor EILEEN LE BRETON

Reader in French Language and Literature,
Bedford College University of London

This series is designed to provide students and general readers both with Monographs on important nineteenth- and twentieth-century French poets and Critical Editions of representative works by these poets.

The Monographs aim at presenting the essential biographical facts while placing the poet in his social and intellectual context. They contain a detailed analysis of his poetical works and, where appropriate, a brief account of his other writings. His literary reputation is examined and his contribution to the development of French poetry is assessed, as is also his impact on other literatures. A selection of critical views and a bibliography are appended.

The Critical Editions contain a substantial introduction aimed at presenting each work against its historical background as well as studying its genre, structure, themes, style, etc. and highlighting its relevance for today. The text normally given is the complete text of the original edition. It is followed by full commentaries on the poems and annotation of the text, including variant readings when these are of real significance, and a select bibliography.

E. Le B.

PAUL VERLAINE

Romances
sans Paroles

edited by
D. HILLERY

UNIVERSITY OF LONDON
THE ATHLONE PRESS
1976

Published by
THE ATHLONE PRESS
UNIVERSITY OF LONDON
at 4 Gower Street, London WC1

Distributed by
Tiptree Book Services Ltd
Tiptree, Essex

U.S.A. and Canada
Humanities Press Inc
New Jersey

Printed in Great Britain by
The Garden City Press Limited
Letchworth, Hertfordshire
SG6 1JS

CONTENTS

INTRODUCTION

BIOGRAPHICAL BACKGROUND

The period which is relevant to the writing and publication of *Romances sans paroles*, allowing a generous margin at the beginning in order better to get the circumstances of the volume's creation into perspective, is that which follows the appearance of *La Bonne Chanson* (Lemerre) on 12 June 1870 and which covers the best part of four years to the appearance of *Romances sans paroles* itself towards the end of March 1874. The day of publication is not known with absolute certainty. The fact that the volume appeared at all was due to the efforts of Verlaine's friend and eventual biographer Edmond Lepelletier who managed to arrange for it to be printed at Sens on the presses of Maurice l'Hermite. Lepelletier, who worked for the republican newspaper *Le Peuple souverain*, had been obliged to leave Paris because of his active sympathy for the Paris Commune; the printing of Verlaine's poems was consequently delayed and was not begun until some time in November 1873. The only reason their approximate date of publication is known is because Verlaine wrote to Lepelletier from prison on 27 March 1874 to thank him for the copies he had been sent: 'Cher ami, reçu lettre et volumes. Merci bien cordialement. Très content de l'aspect et de la confection du petit bouquin. L'air un peu *brochure* peut-être,— mais c'est très respectable. Pas trop de coquilles . . . très reconnaissant des soins apportés. Vienne maintenant l'acheteur! (Il est prudent d'employer le singulier, quand il s'agit d'un article aussi peu de vente que des vers) . . .'. In the hope of finding a possible clientele, Verlaine, in July of the previous year, had drawn up a list of journalists and writers to whom copies should be sent for review. Lepelletier, apparently, did as Verlaine wished: 'je fis un service aux journaux très complet. Pas un ne cita même le titre du livre'. That was not entirely correct. One solitary review did find its way to the light of day in the *Rappel* of 16 April 1874. Its author was another of Verlaine's closest friends Emile Blémont (in reality Léon-Emile Petitdidier). The text is worth quoting in full: 'Nous venons de recevoir les *Romances sans paroles* de Paul Verlaine. C'est encore de la musique, musique souvent bizarre, triste toujours, et qui semble l'écho de mystérieuses douleurs. Parfois une singulière originalité, parfois une malheureuse affectation de naïveté et de morbidesse. Voici une des plus jolies mélodies de ces *Romances*.

> Le piano que baise une main frêle
> Luit dans le soir rose et gris vaguement,
> Tandis qu'avec un très léger bruit d'aile
> Un air bien vieux, bien faible et bien charmant
> Rôde discret, épeuré quasiment,
> Par le boudoir longtemps parfumé d'Elle

Cela n'est-il pas musical, très musical, maladivement musical? Il ne faut pas s'attarder dans ce boudoir'. On that limp and perfunctory note the review ends. Blémont's choice of poem was not very careful since readers of the *Renaissance littéraire et artistique*, to which he was a regular contributor, would have been familiar with the 'ariette' from its publication two years previously in that same periodical. At best Blémont could be said to have done his duty—presumably out of a sense of friendship and loyalty to Verlaine—but he offers no evidence to show that he had read the poems in any detail nor that he had understood them, even though he ought to have been familiar with them from Verlaine's correspondence.

There followed a long period of complete silence. The original edition was never sold and it was not until a second edition was brought out in 1887, by which time Verlaine had acquired a reputation and a following, that *Romances sans paroles* found its readership and earned its relative popularity. Verlaine, in the article on himself in the series *Les Hommes d'aujourd'hui*, confirms this, calling *Romances sans paroles* 'son volume peut-être le plus original, mais qui devait beaucoup plus tard faire son bruit dans le nouveau monde poétique' ('Prose', p. 766). It seems an odd quirk of fate that this slim volume, so carefully prepared and so urgently championed by its author, a volume coming out of one of the most turbulent and unsettled periods of his life, should have gone unnoticed for so long. Perhaps unnoticed is not the right word; it might be more accurate to say ignored. The silence which descended on Verlaine and his work was not the result of a disinterested decision based on artistic merit, it was very largely a question of moral opprobrium. This particular bias was most blatantly illustrated on the occasion of Verlaine submitting a selection of poems for inclusion in the third volume of the *Parnasse contemporain* in 1875. Anatole France is reported to have said, among other things, 'non. L'auteur est indigne'.[1]

1870 If *La Bonne Chanson* is a reliable guide to Verlaine's approach to his marriage which no doubt to some extent it is—though for a rather different, if complementary, attitude see the 'Vieilles Bonnes Chansons' where the anticipation is overtly sexual—then he would seem to have regarded the marriage as a refuge from his own disturbingly insecure temperament and as a means of overcoming his unfortunate liking for alcohol. If that is only partially true Verlaine, as it turned out, was singularly mistaken in his expectations. Had he exhibited in 1870 the more realistic sentiments apparent in 'Child Wife' (cant apart) three years later, he would never have assumed that a sixteen-year-old girl was capable of transforming him into the model of domesticity and reasonableness which he seemed to want to become. Nor would he have ever imagined that he himself was capable of sloughing off the more undesirable traits of his temperament and of donning permanently the evidently tempting cloak of respectability.[2]

To begin with, the marriage does not appear to have been entirely unsuccessful. After a week with Mathilde's parents in the rue Nicolet the couple moved to an apartment on the quai de la Tournelle—Mathilde's choice—and furnished it; again it was Mathilde's taste which dictated the decoration: pink chintz, various pieces of antique furniture and a Pleyel grand piano (Mathilde's mother was a pianist of some distinction; she may have been a pupil of Chopin—evidence suggests she was not—but she certainly taught the young Debussy). Verlaine had a routine job at the Hôtel de Ville in which he took but little interest. In one respect, however, totally outside the influence of both Mathilde and Verlaine, the marriage had come at an unfortunate time. The Franco-Prussian war had been declared on 15 July. By 11 August, the wedding day, Paris was already under threat of siege. The siege proper began in mid-September and would not be lifted until the following January. Verlaine was called up to do his national service in conditions which he could not have foreseen and which he would certainly not have chosen (for an account of his military prowess, or lack of it, Joanna Richardson's *Verlaine* is quite instructive). The combination of a humdrum existence at work, the lack of intellectual stimulus at home, the attraction of evenings away on duty was soon sufficient to draw Verlaine back to heavy bouts of drinking. At this stage in his life he was comfortably off and quite able to afford to indulge in his passion for alcohol. For the time being his drunkenness is only occasional, but there are reasons enough to believe that even infrequent drinking sessions were a cause of friction between him and Mathilde. The ideals of *La Bonne Chanson* were fast disappearing; but though the marriage was not prospering it was by no means on the point of disintegration.

One small yet important item seems worth mentioning. While still at the lycée, Verlaine had struck up a friendship with Lucien Viotti, a young man some years his junior. The relationship, at least from Verlaine's side, was something more than normal friendship and evidently contained elements of homosexual attraction. At the time of Verlaine's marriage the relationship was still close, how close it is impossible to say. At the outbreak of hostilities with Prussia Viotti joined up. He was killed on 29 November 1870. How far his death affected Verlaine at the time it is difficult to judge, but in 1885 in the periodical *Lutèce* of 1–8 February, Verlaine published a short piece entitled 'Les Mémoires d'un veuf. A la mémoire de mon Lucien Viotti'—later changed to 'A la mémoire de mon ami ***'—where the sentiments expressed leave little room for doubt: 'tout ton être élégant et fin de vingt ans, ta tête charmante... les exquises proportions de ton corps d'éphèbe sous le costume de gentleman, m'apparaît à travers mes larmes lentes à couler' ('lentes' because he dared not show his feelings in 1870?). Equally significant, the original ending of the piece was 'tu mourus . . . à cause de moi qui ne valait pas une goutte de ton sang, pour celle [unquestionably a disparaging reference to Mathilde] qui ne me vaut même pas'. This particular conclusion was arrived at with all the advantages of hindsight and does not necessarily represent an accurate reflection of Verlaine's feelings at the end of 1870, but it is none the less very unlikely that Verlaine remained unaffected by his companion's death and equally unlikely that he did not make some sort of comparison between his relationship with Mathilde and his friendship with Viotti.

1871 The historical/political events of 1871 were disturbing for Verlaine and Mathilde. On 28 January Paris capitulated to the Prussians and one month later, 26 February, Thiers signed the peace treaty with Bismarck. On 1 March Prussian troops entered the city, but by 18 March the Commune had seized power and Paris was once more in a state of siege, this time from French troops of the newly formed Versailles government. Verlaine found himself, along with his friends—especially Lepelletier—supporting the Commune. At that time his political beliefs were rather left of centre—he seems to have mustered some enthusiasm for the Republic—but as he got older they were to become more and more right wing. On 10 May the Treaty of Frankfurt signalled the official end of the war. Shortly afterwards, on 28 May, the Commune was overthrown. Lepelletier went into temporary hiding. Verlaine decided it was prudent to leave Paris and went with Mathilde, who was by then pregnant, to Fampoux. On 11 July the Prefect of the Seine dismissed Verlaine and his colleagues from their posts at the Hôtel de Ville. This was the only specifically political reprisal, if indeed one can go that far, which was taken against Verlaine, and even in this instance he himself was not singled out for special attention. Yet as a result he continued to feel insecure about his presence in France for a good many years. However, in August, Verlaine and Mathilde returned to Paris. It was decided that they should give up their flat on the quai de la Tournelle and move into the second floor of Mathilde's parents' house in the rue Nicolet. Verlaine, who was without a job, showed no interest in obtaining one. Also, he appears to have spent as much time as he could away from the house. Into this undoubtedly unpromising situation Verlaine would go out of his way to invite Rimbaud—initially, let it be said, for purely literary reasons (coloured by a touch of vanity)—and, once he had arrived, to keep him. On the literary side the reasons were pressing. There are letters to Léon Valade and to Blémont in which Verlaine confesses that he has virtually stopped writing poetry, 'd'ailleurs, je travaille peu' (14 July); 'pour moi je deviens paresseux' (29 July). It is difficult to interpret the lack of work except as a sign that something was fairly seriously amiss. And on the purely domestic level the situation was slowly deteriorating. On hearing of Blémont's forthcoming marriage, Verlaine had written to congratulate him and had added, 'je n'ai pas, quant à moi, à me plaindre du mien' (13 July). All was by no means as satisfactory as Verlaine implied. Mathilde's half brother Charles de Sivry, who had done a lot on Verlaine's behalf prior to the engagement to Mathilde, had stayed with the couple in April and had witnessed Verlaine's violent temper and irascibility towards his wife. The same violence was to flare up with increasing frequency after Rimbaud's arrival; and it would appear that Rimbaud played some part in encouraging this side of Verlaine's nature.

In September Rimbaud arrived in Paris. Verlaine's famous invitation, 'venez, chère grande âme, on vous appelle, on vous attend', was promptly responded to. From the point of view of Verlaine's marriage Rimbaud's presence was disastrous. Verlaine drank more, was more frequently drunk and more frequently violent (for Mathilde's account of the period see her *Mémoires*). He also managed to alienate a good many of his acquaintances. Lepelletier, whose biography is as favourable to Verlaine as it is possible to be, detested Rimbaud and is on record as having commented, on the occasion of a visit by Verlaine and Rimbaud to a play of François Coppée's, on Verlaine 'giving his arm to a charming young lady, Mlle Rimbaud'. Rimbaud made himself so objectionable that he was soon asked to move from the Mauté household. He stayed subsequently with various of Verlaine's artist friends until they too were reluctant to entertain him longer.

On 30 October Georges Verlaine was born. It cannot be said that Verlaine was a model of paternal understanding, for the child, in turn, became the object of the poet's outbursts of uncontrollable rage. 1871 ended in an atmosphere of domestic tension and even hostility with Verlaine regarded, and acting, as something of an outcast.

1872 Brief weeks excepted, the relationship between Verlaine and his wife grew steadily more intolerable. In *Romances sans paroles* Verlaine blames Mathilde for the way things turned out, but it is perfectly clear that Verlaine himself must take a large share of the responsibility for the ultimate breakdown of the marriage. Yet another violent physical attack on Mathilde and Georges, in January, had had as its result the departure of Mathilde, Georges and M. Mauté to Périgueux where they remained for six weeks. Mathilde agreed to return to Paris but only on condition that Rimbaud was sent away; yet it was in the end necessary for her to threaten to begin proceedings in view of obtaining legal separation (there was no divorce at that date) in order to persuade Verlaine to do as she wanted. The two months or so following her return were relatively stable and peaceful. Rimbaud, however, returned in May.

The separation of Verlaine and Rimbaud had not been complete. They had succeeded in maintaining a fairly regular correspondence, a certain amount of which is still available (on this point see Antoine Adam's new edition of Rimbaud's work published by Gallimard, 'Pléiade' in 1972). For example, Verlaine had written to Rimbaud to thank him for the Favart *ariette* (see the commentary to the first 'Ariette oubliée' p. 71) on 2 April. Judging by the tone of the letter the relationship between the two men had not suffered, and a letter in May beginning: 'Cher Rimbe bien gentil' can leave no doubt at all concerning the closeness of the friendship. At least it had a positive result in terms of Verlaine's poetry for it was in May that he started to publish some of the *Romances sans paroles* in the *Renaissance littéraire et artistique* (see the commentaries to the first and fifth of the 'Ariettes oubliées' p. 71 and p. 78 respectively). Within two months, on 7 July, without prior warning Verlaine abandoned Mathilde and set off on his peregrinations with Rimbaud to Belgium and, eventually, London. The same month he wrote to Lepelletier, 'Je voillage vertigineusement'.

Contrary to what one might have expected, Mathilde decided to go to Brussels to try to persuade Verlaine to return with her to Paris, Verlaine having written to her in a manner which indicated that his desertion was only temporary. She—and her mother—arrived in Brussels on 22 July. As far as one can gather, there was an ecstatic reunion, an echo of which can be heard in 'Birds in the Night'; Verlaine began the journey back, but at the frontier station of Quiévrain he refused to go any further. As far as can be ascertained that was the last time Verlaine and Mathilde were to see each other.

August was spent wandering round Belgium with Rimbaud. On 7 September the pair embarked at Ostend for Dover arriving in London on the 9th (?) where they managed to find rooms off Tottenham Court Road at 35 Howland Street.

By this date, two of the 'Ariettes oubliées' had been published and the others, in all probability, written. The 'Paysages Belges' had also been composed. From now until the end of the year Verlaine's main preoccupations will be his relationship with Mathilde and his plans for the publication of the volume of poetry which will eventually be called *Romances sans paroles*, though to give it a title at this point is to anticipate Verlaine's decision by a few weeks. With regard to Mathilde, Verlaine was torn between a sense of outrage at *his* having been deserted and an evidently equally strong desire to emphasise Mathilde's less attractive characteristics in an attempt to excuse, if only partially, his conduct. A letter to Lepelletier in September suggests that his wife's 'vraie nature', as Verlaine sees it, is '*pratique* et bavarde . . . à l'excès'. Yet he can go on to write immediately after this: 'le fait est que je suis horriblement triste, car j'aime ma femme trop . . . je désire ardemment que ma femme revienne à moi'. His only condition is that they should no longer live with Mathilde's parents because that had been a situation which, for whatever reason, he had found intolerable. The same letter carries a P.S., 'à une proche occase, t'écrirai très curieux détails pittoresques et enverrai vers nouveau-modèle très bien . . .'. This could be a reference to work already done, possibly the 'Paysages Belges', though it could equally be meant to refer to some other poetic project (Verlaine's 'impersonal' poetry?). As is so often the case with Verlaine, he does not specify what he means. Further letters of the same month, to Lepelletier, contain fairly detailed descriptions of London scenes and a personal and somewhat insulting dig at Leconte de Lisle—'Ah par exemple, on y bafoue les Jésuites, et je "ne sais comment" les pitres chargés de cette exécution ressemblent tous à Leconte de Lisle:

c'est inouï de ressemblance!' (After the Paris Commune the
relationship between the two poets was never more than cool.
Verlaine wrote a couple of articles on Leconte de Lisle, one in
the series *Les Hommes d'aujourd'hui* and one entitled 'Souvenirs sur
Leconte de Lisle' (1894). Neither piece is hostile. On the other
hand, in the poems of *Invectives*, published posthumously by
Vanier in 1896, the 'Portrait Académique' is of a totally different
tone:

> Fleur de cuistrerie et de méchanceté
> Au parfum de lucre et de servilité,
> Et poussée en plein terrain d'Hypocrisie . . .

It may well represent Verlaine's personal feelings towards
Leconte de Lisle. It does not prevent him from admiring the
poetry). Tantalising as ever, the same letter contains the
unidentified and unidentifiable 'ci-joint un poème nouveau'
(part of 'Birds in the Night'?). To Blémont, on 22 September,
Verlaine was more specific: 'enfin je travaille beaucoup ici . . .'
and he enclosed some poems 'pour une série que je nommerais:
De Charleroi à Londres'. The poems Verlaine included were
'Simple Fresque' ('La fuite est verdâtre et rose'), 'Paysage Belge'
('L'allée est sans fin'), 'Chevaux de Bois' and—inexplicably?—
'Escarpolette' ('Je devine à travers un murmure'). 'Escarpolette'
had been composed in May and, chronologically at least, had
nothing to do with the period after Verlaine's desertion of
Mathilde, or so Verlaine's dating implies (see p. 104).

Two days later, 24 September, a letter to Lepelletier offered
even more information about Verlaine's plans. Apart from ex-
pressing his admiration for the London docks, which, he said
'suffisent . . . à ma poétique de plus en plus *moderniste*', the letter
revealed that Verlaine had decided to publish the poems he had
been working on: 'Ci-joints deux petits poèmes [again, there are
no details] à la suite de celui que je t'ai envoyé: je me propose de
les faire imprimer, avec d'autres (congénères et d'un tout autre
genre) sous le titre de *Romances sans paroles*, ici, dans un mois: je
compte sur toi pour réclames'. Verlaine's connections with
Vermersch, whose periodical *L'Avenir* had Verlaine's collabor-
ation, gave him the idea that publication of his poems would be
a quick and easy task. (On 2 October Mathilde petitioned for

separation. On 4 October Verlaine wrote to Victor Hugo to ask
him to intercede with Mathilde on his behalf. 'C'est moi le
quitté . . .'). The letter of 5 October to Blémont confirms the title
of the collection and seems to imply that the volume is ready for
the printer, though what it consists of at this date in addition to
the 'Ariettes oubliées' and the 'Paysages Belges' is impossible to
tell with any accuracy: 'Mon petit volume est intitulé: *Romances
sans paroles*; une dizaine de petits poèmes pourraient en effet se
dénommer: "Mauvaise Chanson". Mais l'ensemble est une série
d'impressions vagues, tristes et gaies, avec un peu de pittoresque
presque naïf: ainsi les "Paysages Belges". Je ne crois pas qu'il y
ait rien d'anglais'. Does the last sentence mean that none of the
'Aquarelles' is written? Or does the reference to a possible
'Mauvaise Chanson' ('une *dizaine* de petits poèmes') imply the
existence of more poems other than the seven sections of 'Birds in
the Night' (even assuming that they are all written; the letter
quotes no more than the first three *douzains*)? 'Spleen' may have
been written by this date and 'Streets I' as well; but that is pure
conjecture. If Verlaine is to be believed then 'Child Wife', the
most obvious candidate for a place in a section called 'Mauvaise
Chanson', is not yet even thought of, since he dates it 2 April
1873.

Between the bouts of feverish poetic activity Verlaine con-
tinued to protest his innocence with regard to his behaviour
towards Mathilde and, for good measure, continued to curse her
parents, or more accurately her father, for Verlaine was always
to retain a certain amount of genuine affection for Mme Mauté.
But his marital worries, at this date, took second place to his
hopes for his volume of poetry. By 8 November he had taken
a further step in the publishing direction and told Lepelletier:
'hier je me suis mis en rapport avec un éditeur et j'espère avant
trois semaines [que] je pourrai envoyer à quelques rares amis,
dont toi, naturellement, une petite plaquette, avec (peut-être)
une eau-forte initiale, intitulée: *Romances sans paroles*'. Verlaine's
estimated three weeks proved to be hopelessly optimistic. In
early December the project was still unfinished. 'Je fais imprimer
ici un petit volume *Romances sans paroles*' he informed Blémont.
Round about the same date, i.e. early December (the exact dates
are not known), another letter to Lepelletier provided much

greater clarification concerning the composition of the volume:
'Je vais porter chez l'imprimeur les *Romances sans paroles* 4
parties:
"Romances sans paroles" [to become "Ariettes oubliées"]
"Paysages Belges"
"Nuit falote" (XVIIIe siècle populaire)
"Birds in the night", avec ceci pour épigraphe:

> En robe grise . . .
> . . . redouter d'embûches
> (INCONNU)

400 vers à peu près en tout: tu auras ça dès paru, c'est-à-dire en
janvier 73'. Yet again Verlaine's optimism was to prove un-
founded and the volume was to receive further modification;
'Nuit falote' would disappear ('Ariette oubliée' vi would seem to
be its sole surviving remnant—assuming there were in fact other
poems in the section) and 'Aquarelles' would become the fourth
and final section of the volume.

The relationship with Rimbaud was turning sour. The youn-
ger poet, growing tired of Verlaine no doubt, decided to leave
London around the beginning of December. With Rimbaud
gone, Verlaine found life difficult to bear. He complained both
to Lepelletier: 'bien triste pourtant: tout seul. R . . . n'est plus là.
Vide affreux!', and to Blémont: 'je suis *mourant* de chagrin, de
maladie, d'ennui, d'abandon'. He seems to have become gen-
uinely ill, however, and was forced to send a telegram for both
his mother and Mathilde.

1873 Not unexpectedly, only Verlaine's mother arrived in
London, accompanied by one of Verlaine's female cousins. Rim-
baud too returned, with funds provided by Verlaine's mother
and doubtless at her instigation. Verlaine recovered and soon
took a renewed interest in *Romances sans paroles*. At the end of
January, or possibly at the beginning of February, in another
letter to Lepelletier, he announced: 'je m'occupe de mon petit
volume. Seulement j'aurais besoin d'un *type*. Veuille donc m'ach-
eter un exemplaire des *Fêtes Galantes* et me l'envoyer vite'. If
Verlaine was by then showing a little impatience with the speed
at which his plans were progressing, that fact alone cannot

account entirely for the tone of a letter to Blémont on 17 February: 'Vous recevrez bientôt mon petit bouquin, peut-être posthume'. Humour apart, there were signs that the *ménage* with Rimbaud was becoming less and less satisfactory, but it was not something to which Verlaine usually alluded in his letters to his friends. The blame for the tardiness of the appearance of *Romances sans paroles* was by no means all Verlaine's. Lepelletier either took an inordinate time to procure a copy of *Fêtes Galantes* or he simply did not try hard enough. Near the end of February Verlaine wrote to him again to remind him of the request: 'je n'attends que les *Fêtes Galantes* pour livrer mon bouquin à l'imprimeur. Veuille me les envoyer au plus vite'. A little later, probably in early March, he was forced to make the same request to Blémont: 'mon petit volume *Romances sans paroles* est archifini [not quite, in fact; "Child Wife", "A Poor Young Shepherd" and "Beams", if nothing else, were still to be written] et n'attend plus que de faire gémir les presses de Greek Street, Soho. Ce que j'attends, moi, c'est un exemplaire des *Fêtes Galantes* (pour servir de type), que Lepelletier doit m'envoyer depuis 15 jours . . .'. Would Blémont send him a copy? But the plans went awry. The projected printing in London, which had appeared one of the most firmly fixed parts of the idea, fell through. So Verlaine was without a printer. On 4 April he and Rimbaud left England to go, for a few weeks, their separate ways; Rimbaud to Roche and Verlaine to Jehonville via Namur, where he was taken ill and where he received letters from Mathilde telling him to stop plaguing her by writing to her so frequently. At Jehonville, Verlaine stayed with his aunt Evrard for about six weeks. During this period there is a fair amount of correspondence concerning Mathilde's impending petition for separation, but by now it is too late for there to be any further effect on the poetry; *Romances sans paroles* is completed.

Once again Verlaine turned his attention to the problem of having the volume published and even printed in Paris. That he should have wanted the poems to be brought out specifically in Paris is not surprising, for only in the capital could he hope to find a sufficient number of readers and reviewers to keep his *poetic* reputation alive. He himself, of course, was most unwilling to return to France—partly because he feared the consequences of his adherence, slight though it was, to the Commune, and partly because of the scandal attached to his relationship with Rimbaud—and had to depend on Lepelletier. But Lepelletier was making no progress. *Romances sans paroles*, had Verlaine's optimism proved correct, should have appeared some months previously—though admittedly the delay enabled Verlaine to add the odd poem to 'Aquarelles'. At that point, Verlaine's letters took on a new tone of urgency. He began to see it as imperative that the volume should appear before Mathilde's petition was heard. 'Tu dois comprendre que j'attache beaucoup d'importance à la publication de mon volume avant ce procès. Car, après, ça aurait l'air de vouloir exploiter le retentissement-réclame que ça fera. Donc, pourrai-je . . . faire imprimer vite, très modestement, et avec quelque délai, ou sans, s'il le faut, *468 vers* purement littéraires?' (to Lepelletier, 15 April).

If Verlaine's account is to be accepted at face value *Romances sans paroles* was only a small part, albeit an important part, of his literary output and ambitions at this period. The extent of his activity is revealed in a letter to Blémont dated 22 April: 'outre le petit volume que je compte faire imprimer à Paris, je prépare un recueil de tous les vers que j'ai inédits (sonnets, vieux poèmes saturniens, vers politiques, et quelques obscénités) . . . je m'occupe aussi d'un drame en prose et d'un grand roman intime (rien d'autobiographique: fi, l'horreur!)'. The 'sonnets, vieux poèmes saturniens' etc. were presumably pieces which would eventually be resurrected to form parts of *Jadis et Naguère* and *Parallèlement*. The same letter contained a copy of 'A Poor Young Shepherd' and 'The Child Wife' (the definite article would be dropped) with the information that they came from a section called 'Aquarelles', 'une partie anglaise'. Evidently Verlaine had changed his mind since 5 October 1872 about the 'English' bit and had also modified his plan of December of that year. Even by April it was not totally clear what the exact state of the volume was, though it seems highly probable that it had been given its final form. On the other hand there was an inexplicably long delay before Verlaine sent the manuscript to Lepelletier, which he did in the middle of May. He may have used the time for revision, or he may simply not have got around to copying it out. On 16 May the manuscript was about to be sent off: 'tu recevras mardi ou mercredi le manuscrit. Avant de m'en accuser réception, cause un peu à Lechevallier, des prix, etc.' (Verlaine was still financially independent, or rather, dependent on his mother. Up to that date, all his volumes of poetry had been published at his own expense, save the *Poèmes Saturniens*). 'Je voudrais que ça fût du format de *La Bonne Chanson* (ah! m . . . !). Si ça pouvait paraître vite, quelle veine! Enfin je te confie cette enfant: rinds-la hûreuse, rinds-la hûreuse'. Previously, Verlaine had apparently wanted the appearance of the volume to resemble that of *Fêtes Galantes*, at least in so far as the type face was concerned. In fact, both *Fêtes Galantes* and *La Bonne Chanson*, in terms of format, were 'petit in-12'. *Romances sans paroles*, in its first edition, was simply 'in-12'; it was the second edition of 1887 that was 'petit in-12'. Three days later, on 19 May, there were more precise details: 'tu recevras,—en même temps que cette lettre—le phameux manusse . . . C'est très en ordre, très revu . . . Je voudrais bien que ça fut vite fait'. Of considerable importance is Verlaine's insistence on the dedication to Rimbaud. 'Je tiens beaucoup à la dédicace à Rimbaud. D'abord *comme protestation*, puis parce que ces vers ont été faits [possibly an oblique reference to the fact that during the period immediately following his marriage he was poetically unproductive], lui étant là et m'ayant poussé beaucoup à les faire, surtout comme témoignage de reconnaissance . . .'. Verlaine must have been only too well aware that Lepelletier would disapprove strongly of the proposed dedication—which he did. In his next letter Verlaine continued to insist that the dedication should remain, but he gave Lepelletier the option of cutting it out. Lepelletier cannot have hesitated. On the manuscript of *Romances sans paroles* belonging to the Fonds Doucet the dedication is firmly struck out. That apart, Lepelletier must have expressed approval of the volume because Verlaine wrote, 23 May: 'je suis enchanté que mon voluminet t'ait plu, malgré ses "hérésies" de versification [about which see pp. 24–32] . . . A vrai dire je n'en suis pas mécontent, bien que ça soit encore bien en deça de ce que je veux faire. Je ne veux plus que l'effort se fasse sentir et en arrive avec de toutes [*sic*] autres procédés,—une fois mon système bien établi dans ma tête . . .'. Verlaine's 'système' will for ever remain a mystery simply because he adopts his far too frequent habit of not revealing precisely what it is he has in mind.[3] 'Bref, je réfléchis très sérieusement (et bien modestement) à une réforme'. In addition he is by now quite unable to resist the customary unkind comments on Mathilde and her parents; Mathilde is 'une vraie scélérate', her mother a mere 'misérable'; as for her father—'je ne parle pas du vieux pou'.

On 25 May Verlaine and Rimbaud met up again at Bouillon. The day after, they left for London from Anvers. On 27 May they found rooms in Camden Town at 8 Great College Street. Verlaine's fully awakened enthusiasm for writing continued unabated; so too did his gift for correspondence. On 30 May a letter went to Blémont: 'je travaille d'ailleurs beaucoup à des vers dont vous aurez un de ces jours des fragments et que je crois vraiment nouveaux—et à un drame et un roman' (presumably the same pair of the letter of 22 April). Yet three weeks later, or thereabouts (the date is uncertain), Verlaine had to confess to the same correspondent: 'je voudrais vous envoyer des vers. Mais je n'en ai aucun'. It transpires he was too busy learning English and giving French lessons in order to earn enough money to live off. Rimbaud, characteristically, refused to do any work. At about the same date (i.e. around 20 June) Verlaine enquired after the progress of *Romances sans paroles*. 'Que devient Gustave [his name for the manuscript]? Je ne vois pas pourquoi la politique pourrait nuire à ce frêle garçon, voué d'avance à une vente *spéciale* et rare, partant'. Were the political fears Verlaine's or, more understandably, Lepelletier's? The point was not pursued. By his own account, Lepelletier had had no success in placing the manuscript; and as it was to turn out was never able to persuade any of the Paris publishing houses to accept it. That fact alone must account for a part of the silence which greeted its eventual appearance.

Relations with Rimbaud deteriorated. On 3 July Verlaine returned alone to Belgium. The decision to leave Rimbaud was sudden but perhaps not entirely unexpected given the fact that the younger poet was being more objectionable than usual. The departure was followed by a rapid series of letters to Rimbaud, Rimbaud's mother, Lepelletier, Mathilde and his own mother in which he threatened to commit suicide. The letters cover the period 3–6 July. Yet such was Verlaine's instability, a letter to his landlady in London on 7 July left it to be understood that he contemplated returning to his rooms in the near future. By 8 July Verlaine had changed his mind again and a telegram was dispatched to Rimbaud reading: 'Volontaire Espagne. Viens ici. Hôtel Liégeois'. The desire to commit suicide (which may well have been genuine, but then again may not) had been watered down to an apparent wish to enlist in the foreign legion (?). Whatever Verlaine's real intentions regarding his own life, one other intention was clear enough: that of persuading Rimbaud to rejoin him. On the evening of 8 July, Rimbaud arrived in Brussels. The sequel is known and is well documented; on 10 July Verlaine shot at Rimbaud, wounding him slightly in the wrist. The outcome was that Verlaine was condemned to two years in prison and to a fine of 200 francs. With remission for good behaviour he would be released on 16 January 1875.

Romances sans paroles was not forgotten. At the end of July Verlaine gave his mother instructions to pass on to Lepelletier: 'Faire imprimer les *Romances sans paroles*, le plus tôt possible—300 exemplaires—format *Fêtes Galantes*. Le même papier. Couverture légèrement saumon'. On this last item Verlaine's wishes were not respected. The colour of the volume was 'bleu pâle'. It was in the same instructions that Verlaine drew up a list of the reviewers to whom a copy of the poems should be sent. Verlaine continued: 'l'impression de ce volume me sera une grande consolation . . . ce sera comme une résurrection: je lui serai bien reconnaissant qu'il fasse de la dédicace ce qu'il voudra, bien que j'y tienne toujours'. His plea for speedy publication, if not unheeded, went unfulfilled. At the end of August (or the beginning of September, the date is again not certain) he repeated his request in modified terms, directly to Lepelletier: 'Je tiens beaucoup à ce que mon livre paraisse cet hiver. Efforce-t-y.—Si tu ne pouvais, remets le manuscrit à ma mère qui s'en oc-cupera . . .'. A month went by and nothing happened. On 28 September the same request went out once more to Lepelletier: 'ma mère a dû te dire toute l'importance que j'attache à la prompte impression et publication de mon petit livre'. Even so, the project was never hurried along—which is rather odd from the purely printing point of view given the slimness of the volume, a mere 48 pages—and though there were signs of progress,

Verlaine's letter of late October was on much the same lines as previous letters: 'Je te remercie bien de vouloir bien t'occuper de mon petit volume [following Lepelletier's failure to place it with a Paris publisher]. Je tiens beaucoup à ce que ça paraisse cette saison-ci. Tu comprends que, étant bien forcé et résolu à vivre désormais de *ma plume* [which he never quite succeeded in doing; he was poverty-stricken for the last dozen or so years of his life], il est urgent que mon nom ne reste pas absolument oublié pendant ces tristes loisirs'. But forgotten he was by most people. He was, in fact, not drawn back into the public eye until the publication of the 'Art poétique' in *Paris moderne* on 10 November 1882 and the subsequent discussion with Charles Morice in *La Nouvelle Rive gauche* of 8 and 15 December (see Chadwick, p. 115).[4] In the meanwhile, Lepelletier had succeeded in finding a printer, and though a letter from Verlaine of 22 November contained the eternal question: 'Quand le petit livre paraîtra-t-il?', a letter two days later was of a different tone: 'je reçois à l'instant ton petit mot et le spécimen du petit bouquin. —C'est très bien'. Verlaine went on to ask that one or two details be altered in 'Streets II' and in 'Birds in the Night' (see the Commentaries, p. 93 and p. 98) added, 'un mot encore: faudra-t-il envoyer à ma femme? Décide. J'eusse, hélas!—et je parle bien sincèrement—préféré lui faire d'autres vers que les "Birds in the Night" (qui sont l'histoire bien vraie de Bruxelles)'. That was the end of the matter for another four months. Verlaine cannot have seen any further proofs and the volume was published, faults and all, in March 1874.

Nearly two years had elapsed since Blémont had inserted 'C'est l'extase langoureuse' in the *Renaissance littéraire et artistique*. Verlaine's whole way of life, and no doubt his career as a poet, had undergone radical changes. *Romances sans paroles* bears testimony to both, and—the religious vein of *Sagesse* apart—has come to be considered typical of the best (and, possibly, the worst) of Verlaine's output.

LITERARY BACKGROUND

Influencing and being influenced by, borrowing from and imitating, constitute nothing if not normal poetic practice and it in no way diminishes either a poet's originality or his stature to suggest that, in one way or another, he was indebted to other writers. Verlaine is no exception. In the case of *Romances sans paroles* the one influence that is readily acknowledged is that of Rimbaud, 'lui étant là et m'ayant poussé beaucoup à les faire' is Verlaine's own bald recognition of the fact that *Romances sans paroles* owes its existence, in no small measure, to the younger poet's encouragement. Verlaine does not, however, elaborate on the statement; and without any other facts to go on other than Rimbaud's undoubted presence and, presumably, interest—though even here conjecture has already taken over from hard fact—it is not surprising that opinions as to the extent of Rimbaud's influence vary enormously depending, one suspects, on the individual's preference for one or the other poet. Lepelletier, whose personal antipathy to Rimbaud needs no emphasising, categorically states that Rimbaud 'est certainement l'auteur de toutes les misères, morales et physiques, qui accablèrent Verlaine. Lui a-t-il rendu quelque service au point de vue intellectuel? Son influence a-t-elle agi sur le talent du poète des *Romances sans paroles*? La poétique nouvelle de Verlaine est-elle issue de l'intimité avec l'auteur du "Bateau Ivre"? Je ne le pense pas' (pp. 269–70). Rimbaud's influence on Verlaine's *temperament* is roundly denounced, as could be expected, but Lepelletier then goes on to deny any specific *poetic* influence because he considers Verlaine a sufficiently mature poet to have evolved his own style without help from Rimbaud. The view is extreme but understandable from one who had followed closely the evolution of Verlaine's poetry from its very inception. It is a view which cannot be dismissed out of hand simply on account of Lepelletier's obvious bias against Rimbaud. At another extreme, there exists the view that 'c'est bien Rimbaud que suit Verlaine, lorsqu'il dénoue les liens de la syntaxe, substitue l'exclamation à la proposition structurée, laisse passer en désordre dans le champ de sa conscience impressions et sensations' (Robichez, p. 140); 'c'est donc bien vers la poésie *objective* voulue par Rimbaud que va Verlaine' (ibid., p. 142). Even assuming one agrees with the various propositions regarding syntax, disorder, and so on, the opinion is highly exclusive and selective in that it relates practically entirely to the 'Ariettes oubliées' which, if Verlaine's dating is not misleading, were composed during the months of May and June 1872 at a time when Verlaine was still in Paris. Rimbaud was certainly with him a lot of the time, but Rimbaud was not his *sole* poetic contact at that period as he was to become a short while afterwards. The possibility of influence cannot be denied (it would be foolish to pretend it could) but its extent can certainly be questioned—and must be—particularly when another writer assesses the 'Paysages Belges' as 'l'œuvre la plus rimbaldienne de Verlaine par son style, tout en impressions superposées' (Zimmermann, p. 57). Perhaps it would be more acceptable, and maybe more accurate, to adopt a cautious approach, crediting Rimbaud with having revived Verlaine's interest in poetry (most probably true) and then proposing that 'de l'effort de Verlaine pour suivre Rimbaud' [and even that is contentious] 'sont nés quelques essais timides d'hallucinations littéraires: union du rêve et de la réalité, transposition et brouillement des sensations, obscurité de certains symboles' (Zayed, p. 357); but that is not really very helpful since it remains, as indeed do most comparisons, on a fairly general level. It is safer to conclude, as Lepelletier had done in different terms that: 'la part qu'a prise Rimbaud dans la formation de Verlaine est plus d'ordre moral et spirituel que d'ordre littéraire' (p. 366). Since, however, literary influence cannot definitely be excluded, it can be allowed for by admitting the idea that Rimbaud encouraged Verlaine 'dans le sens de son propre [i.e. Verlaine's] génie et de sa propre originalité' (p. 367). To say as much is not to discredit Rimbaud's influence, but it does lead to the thought that Rimbaud and Verlaine had fundamentally irreconcilable attitudes to poetry and, further, it can equally well lead to a line of argument which sees the mood and technical achievements of *Romances sans paroles* as implicit in the *Poèmes Saturniens* and the *Fêtes Galantes*. Once that line of inquiry has been opened up then any specific rimbaldian influence is much harder to trace given the possibility that apparently new elements in Verlaine's poetry could be found, in some form, in the earlier collections. Borel's conclusion is as careful and as non-committal as Zayed's: 'la dette de Verlaine envers Rimbaud, on le voit, est beaucoup moins évidente, beaucoup moins facilement repérable qu'on ne l'a cru et dit. Il s'agit moins d'une influence que d'une incitation' ('Pléiade', p. 177); which in the last analysis, is precisely what Verlaine himself said. Yet the position is not quite so simple. In so far as Rimbaud is believed to have helped to promote the *best* elements in Verlaine's poetry it is argued that he 'saved' Verlaine from following the line of poetic composition and mood exemplified in *La Bonne Chanson*. The opinion is not without its attractions, but rests on two basic assumptions which in themselves are questionable. In the first place the poetry of *La Bonne Chanson* is considered mediocre—which is more a question of taste than of objective fact (see Chadwick, pp. 28–34); in the second place it seems to be accepted that Verlaine would have continued writing in that particular way—which is a matter of pure supposition. *La Bonne Chanson* is exceptional in that it is a volume written for, or arising out of, a well defined set of circumstances. That Rimbaud should have objected to *La Bonne Chanson* and all it stood for can more or less be taken for granted, but that on that account he should be thought to have brought Verlaine back to his poetic senses and that he should be held responsible, in a praiseworthy way, for Verlaine's *poetic* salvation is much too sweeping an assertion. Quite simply, there are no precise details on which to base such an assertion. What mutual exchanges and discussions actually took place, what technical suggestions were actually put into practice—and on that score Verlaine was never less than Rimbaud's equal—will remain a matter for conjecture. That Rimbaud preferred Verlaine to write in a certain manner is probably beyond doubt. That he encouraged Verlaine to develop that manner (by common consent that particular style is confined to the 'Ariettes oubliées' and to the 'Paysages Belges') would have been only natural. Beyond that it is impossible to go with accuracy without seeming to play down Verlaine's real achievement in *Romances sans paroles* and without seeming to suggest that Rimbaud is the greater—and better—poet.

To venture away from Rimbaud is to wander into the field of much less tangible influences—always granting that even after having expressed so many qualifications it is still possible to look upon Rimbaud as a 'major' influence—in which what is being assessed is the general literary climate of the early 1870s. Verlaine was part of it until mid-1872, but after that he remained at best on the fringes. How much he assimilated, how many poets he admired are matters which cannot be determined with any accuracy. To leave the question at Rimbaud, however, would be much too restrictive, because if there is another influence on *Romances sans paroles* that can be mentioned with any confidence then it is that of Marceline Desbordes-Valmore. It may at first sight seem strange to include this little known romantic poet among the recognisable influences; none the less she is the only writer other than Rimbaud to whom Verlaine refers as having been specifically connected with his reading and enthusiasms during the period of composition of *Romances sans paroles*. Yet even here the figure of Rimbaud looms large in the background. Prior to meeting Rimbaud, Verlaine admitted to having known Desbordes-Valmore's poetry only at second hand. It was Rimbaud who 'nous força presque de lire *tout* ce que nous pensions être un fatras avec des beautés dedans. Notre étonnement fut grand . . .' ('Prose', p. 666). The impression her poetry made was obviously long-lasting:

> La plus noble d'esprit, la plus grande de cœur,
> Partant la plus charmante et la plus douloureuse
> Des femmes, c'est encore le poète vainqueur
> Du rhythme souple et sûr et de la rime heureuse.

So begins the second of two poems to Marceline Desbordes-Valmore in Verlaine's collection of poems *Dédicaces* ('Pléiade', pp. 640-2). Both poems are expressions of Verlaine's evidently very sincere regard for her as a writer—'ô sublime poète'—and as a woman—'femme exquise'. She figured as one of his *Poètes maudits* ('Prose', pp. 666–78) and he published an article on her in *Le Figaro* of 8 August 1894 in which he went so far as to refer to her as: 'celle qui m'a ouvert tout un horizon cordial et montré la voie' ('Prose', p. 929). On his own admission the aspects of her poetry to which he was the most sensitive were her 'douleur' and 'passion', her 'paysages' and her ability to manipulate the 'vers impair'. Little encouragement is needed to draw parallels with *Romances sans paroles*. The qualities Verlaine picked out were all common to his own poetry; but what conclusions can be drawn? That *Romances sans paroles* was written as a direct result of

Verlaine's new-found acquaintance with Desbordes-Valmore's poetry is very much open to doubt. On the other hand her influence cannot be discounted. Again, it may be safer to adopt a compromise and suggest that her poetry may have helped develop aspects of Verlaine's poetic genius which were already reasonably fully mature. Her influence was in the nature of a catalyst—no more; but no less.

It would be tempting to stop at that point, but it would mean ignoring the possible influence of poets with whose work Verlaine had long been quite familiar, poets such as Hugo, Sainte-Beuve, Banville, Baudelaire, Leconte de Lisle.[5] Admittedly what one is now writing about is really the question of the *formative* influences on Verlaine and whether there were still discernible traces of them in the later poetry. There can be no doubt that the early poetry, *Poèmes Saturniens* especially, carried more than just the vague flavour of some of the older poets. Verlaine, in his usual cavalier fashion, observed in his *Confessions* (1895) that his *Poèmes Saturniens* were 'du Leconte de Lisle à ma manière, agrémenté de Baudelaire de ma façon'. But that particular sort of acknowledgement finds no corresponding echo for the 1870s. Memories of poets read and enjoyed may well have flitted through Verlaine's mind during the composition of *Romances sans paroles*, but the days of heady flights of admiration and emulation had virtually disappeared. Certainly, the early 1870s saw nothing comparable from Verlaine's pen to the article he had devoted to Baudelaire in *L'Art* of November and December 1865 (see 'Prose', pp. 599–612). Nor were the 1870s (references to his *personal relationships* with his wife and with Rimbaud apart) ever written about in Verlaine's last years with the same friendly nostalgia with which he recalled the era up to and including the *Parnasse contemporain* (1866). For Verlaine those youthful days came to represent a sort of poetic haven to which he returned with increasing pleasure. Hugo had charmed him; '*Les Orientales* me plurent à quinze ans . . . — . . . et me plaisent encore, comme beau travail de bimbeloterie "artistique" ', he wrote in 1890 ('Prose', p. 726); Banville had, apparently, swept him off his feet. In his 'Souvenirs sur Théodore de Banville' (1891) he says that *Les Cariatides* (1842) and *Les Stalactites* (1846) 'frappèrent littéralement d'admiration et de sympathie mes seize ans déjà littéraires . . . ils exercèrent sur moi une influence décisive'. In the *Confessions* he put his admiration for Banville even earlier—to the age of fourteen, at which point, he says, '*Les Cariatides* . . . m'empoigna sur le champ'. There could be no clearer an indication of whole-hearted approval. At the same time there could be no more nebulous an indication to work on with regard to instances of imitation or borrowing as far as *Romances sans paroles* is concerned. Yet, however fragmented its expression, one fact does emerge which links all the poets mentioned and which, in turn, links them (in a very general sense) to any of Verlaine's collections of poems: namely, Verlaine's constant interest in either the 'atmosphere' of the poetry he admires and/or the technical skill it displays. These are Verlaine's touchstones. They remain with him throughout his career and they are derived, the one obviously from his own temperament, the other from the example he discovered in older poets. To that extent, therefore, and *only* to that extent, *Romances sans paroles* could well indeed harbour shades of Hugo, Baudelaire and Banville.

There remains the slightly curious case of Sainte-Beuve. To begin with he falls into the same category as the others. In the article on Baudelaire, Verlaine had reserved some rather flattering comments for a poem called 'Les Rayons jaunes', 'le plus beau poème à coup sûr, de cet admirable recueil *Joseph Delorme*, que pour mon compte je mets, comme intensité de mélancolie et comme puissance d'expression, infiniment au-dessus des jérémiades lamartiniennes et autres' ('Prose', p. 599). The laudatory tone was to remain constant. In the *Poètes maudits* Verlaine refers to him as 'ce merveilleux Sainte-Beuve' ('Prose', p. 666). Perhaps Verlaine's fondness for Sainte-Beuve derives in part from the fact that the older critic's reactions to Verlaine's early poetry had been pleasantly favourable—Verlaine wrote of his 'critiques bienveillantes'—but there can be no real doubt that Verlaine had a sincere regard for *Joseph Delorme* both on account of its personal, confessional mood and on account of the ideas on poetry contained in the 'Pensées de Joseph Delorme' (particularly the emphasis on form). It might have been concluded, therefore, that Sainte-Beuve's influence was much in line with that of the previously mentioned poets. There exists, however, an odd piece of information that cannot be entirely overlooked: Charles Morice, in his *Paul Verlaine*, lays some emphasis on the debt owed to Sainte-Beuve and links the rhythmic variety and experimentation of *Romances sans paroles* with Sainte-Beuve's example (see pp. 53-4). It could be that Morice was simply expressing a personal opinion. On the other hand it is just possible that Verlaine himself may have expressed this view to Morice in conversation or in correspondence. Unfortunately there is no way of finding out.

By 1872-3, let it be said in conclusion, Verlaine was his own poetic master. Outside sources and influences, where they operate at all, operate in a way which is practically untraceable. Their presence may be no less real for that, but it cannot be accurately charted.[6]

THE ART OF 'ROMANCES SANS PAROLES'

(i) *Technique*

One of the supposedly striking features of *Romances sans paroles* is its originality, a quality which even the poet himself recognised when he wrote of it as 'un volume dont on a parlé, depuis, beaucoup, car il contenait plusieurs parties assez nouvelles' ('Prose', p. 688), or as 'son volume peut-être le plus original' (ibid., p. 766). That is all very well, but a problem arises when it has to be decided what particular features are indeed the most original. Two connected areas which have been most frequently remarked on are those of rhythm and rhyme. One general word of caution needs uttering at the outset (it has been uttered on numerous previous occasions): the idea of originality must not be pushed too far; Verlaine always worked within an established framework. It is a framework he never ignored no matter how freely he happened to treat it. Therefore, originality does not consist of innovation but of modification of existing practice and of exploitation of existing possibilities.

It may seem premature to announce it at this juncture, but rhythmically *Romances sans paroles*, in a strictly historical sense, offers nothing new. All its basic rhythms have been used before, though not necessarily by Verlaine and not necessarily with the same expertise. The main reason the rhythms of *Romances sans paroles*, in themselves not as interesting as sections of the *Poèmes Saturniens* and *Sagesse*, have received such attention is because of the 'Art poétique'. This by now notorious poem has become unavoidably linked with *Romances sans paroles*, partly because of its date of composition—April 1874—and partly because the principles it advocates are best seen in the 'Ariettes oubliées'.

> De la musique avant toute chose
> Et pour cela préfère l'Impair . . .

It is on those few words that the rhythmic 'novelty' of *Romances sans paroles* rests, since in terms of its use of the *impair* it certainly practises what the 'Art poétique' preaches. Yet even on this count, and granted that *Romances sans paroles* contains a relatively high proportion of *vers impairs*, a down-to-earth perspective is called for as a corrective to too exalted a view of the importance of the *impair*. As a whole *Romances sans paroles* contains a minority of that particular form. The section 'Birds in the Night', eighty-four lines in all, is written entirely in decasyllables; 'Aquarelles' can only boast 'A Poor Young Shepherd' in *impair* (one poem out of seven). 'Ariettes oubliées', on the other hand, has four poems in *impair* (i, ii, iv, viii) and one shared (ix); while the 'Paysages Belges' has three (the poems which make up the section 'Bruxelles') out of six. Of the poems in *impair*, ignoring the mixture in 'Ariettes oubliées' ix, three are in lines of five syllables, two in lines of seven, another two in lines of nine and one in lines of eleven syllables, the 'Ariette oubliée' iv. Verlaine himself only ever comments on this last in his article on Marceline Desbordes-Valmore, and then only briefly to the effect that it is 'inusité'. His own most notable use of it occurs in the poem 'Crimen Amoris' from *Jadis et Naguère*. The nine syllable line is, of course, used for the 'Art poétique' itself.

It is immediately clear that the only sense in which it can be said that the *vers impair* in *Romances sans paroles* is exceptional is in its *concentration* within the two opening sections. For his own part Verlaine is not trying out a new form. He had exhibited his ability in that direction in the *Poèmes Saturniens* (see 'Marine', 'Soleils couchants' and 'La Chanson des Ingénues'). He would continue to show no less consummate a skill in its manipulation much later in 1891 in the *Chansons pour Elle* where six of the twenty-five poems are in *impair*. It is extremely doubtful, however, whether such elevated sentiments as

> Lorsque tu cherches tes puces
> C'est très rigolo (xxi)

or

> Chemise de femme, armure *ad hoc*
> Pour les chers combats et le gai choc (xv)

would qualify for the particular brand of music that the 'Art poétique' advocates. The *impair*

> Plus vague et plus soluble dans l'air,
> Sans rien en lui qui pèse ou qui pose

seems singularly inappropriate in the context of Verlaine's guardian angel Eugénie Krantz.

There is a further point connected with rhythmic variation, namely, the longer the line the greater the variation possible; and it is a fact that the alexandrine is the line into which the greatest number of rhythmic subtleties can be introduced. In the last analysis the distinction between the five syllables of

> Dans l'interminable
> Ennui de la plaine

and the six of, say, 'A Clymène' (*Fêtes Galantes*):

> Mystiques barcarolles,
> Romances sans paroles

or indeed the four of 'Charleroi':

> Dans l'herbe noire
> Les Kobolds vont,

while quite apparent to an ear more accustomed to a line with an even number of syllables would none the less not have meant a great deal simply because the line of five syllables is *short*. The shorter the line, the more the emphasis is thrown on to the rhyme and the more the irregularity of the uneven number of syllables is offset by the short interval between each rhyme word. The line of five syllables is as much a jingle (in no pejorative sense) as is any other short line. The fact that it is a *vers impair* confers on it no special status, except that of infrequent occurrence. It is only in the longer lines of seven and more especially nine and eleven syllables that the relatively unusual metre can be held to produce any readily interesting or distinguishable effect; and then it does so mainly by virtue of the comparison with the more customary lines of eight, ten or twelve syllables. To suggest, as Verlaine does (or as he appears to; it depends how seriously the 'Art poétique' is taken), that the *impair* is more 'musical' is to show a fair amount of imagination. The 'musical' qualities of the *impair* are simply not intrinsic unless an odd number of syllables is equated with musicality; but if they were, the *Chansons pour Elle* would have to be considered on a par with the 'Ariettes oubliées' and the 'Paysages Belges'—which they have every right to be from a purely rhythmical point of view. What distinguishes them from the 'Ariettes oubliées' is their content. It is the 'vrai vague' of the 'Ariettes oubliées' that is of crucial importance, not the fact that some of them are in *vers impairs*, because no amount of argument could establish beyond reasonable doubt that 'C'est l'extase langoureuse' is any more musical than 'Il pleure dans mon cœur' or that 'Il faut, voyez-vous, nous pardonner les choses' scores in that respect over 'Le piano que baise une main frêle'. The point is not without relevance in the context of originality. It is clear enough that none of the poems is original in the sense that it is written in a hitherto unused metre. On the other hand one cannot dispute the remarkable rhythmical variety of *Romances sans paroles*. In what is only a slim volume of twenty-three poems ('Birds in the Night' counting as a single poem) Verlaine uses every available metre from four to twelve syllables inclusive. Few poets are as consciously 'different' as that; but variety does not necessarily constitute originality.

A further point of some importance, judging by the attention that has been given to it, is the part played in the rhythmic variations of *Romances sans paroles* by the mute 'e'. Zimmermann has drawn from its use in the 'Ariettes oubliées' the conclusion that it is of considerable help in the establishing of a vague mood. Nadal, writing of Verlaine's poetry in general, says: 'Il est certain que l'emploi de l'*e* muet placé comme un suspens dans le martèlement régulier du vers a fini par avoir raison de l'heureuse sécurité du mètre pair et des parfaites symétries de ses coupes' (p. 149). The main thing that concerns the degree of importance is obviously the frequency with which the mute 'e' is used (the elided 'e' as in 'Que l'herb*e* agité*e* expire' can be discounted; it is the mute 'e' as a syllable that matters: for example 'Vain*es* précautions! cruell*e* destinée' (*Phèdre*, I. III)). Immediately it is a question of statistics—distasteful though that may seem. As far as each separate section of the collection is concerned, statistics are not especially helpful: that the 'Paysages Belges' has a higher proportion of mute 'e's than the 'Ariettes oubliées' is not particularly significant; that 'Birds in the Night' is poorly endowed with them might, if one were inclined to interpret the result according to one's assessment of the poetic quality of that particular section, indicate that it is less good than the other sections; that 'Aquarelles' has a higher proportion than 'Birds in the Night' does not come as a surprise. Of more interest is the use within individual poems or even individual stanzas. But here, Verlaine shows neither consistency nor development. From his very earliest published poems he exhibits a familiarity with the mute 'e' which later poems do not surpass. 'Mon rêve familier' (*Poèmes Saturniens*) contains the extraordinary line, 'Est-ell*e* brun*e*, blonde ou rouss*e*?—Je l'ignore'; 'Un Dahlia', more conventionally, contains, 'Déroul*e*, mat*e*, ses impeccabl*es* accords', and the opening verse of 'Femme et Chatte', more conventional still, achieves a fair concentration of mute 'e's:

> Ell*e* jouait avec sa chatte,
> Et c'était merveill*e* de voir
> La main blanche et la blanch*e* patte
> S'ébattr*e* dans l'ombr*e* du soir.

Neither the 'Ariettes oubliées' nor the 'Paysages Belges' uses the mute 'e' in ways which are markedly different or more concentrated than that. If instances of its use were to be singled out, then the last verse of 'Ariette oubliée' i (p. 51), the whole of 'Ariette oubliée' ix (p. 56), 'Walcourt' (p. 57) and 'Malines' (p. 61) could be mentioned; even so, it is difficult to see what conclusions could be drawn, given the differences in the poems themselves. In the last resort, the importance of the mute 'e' lies in its application in the individual poem (or line), initially in connection with the rhythm (and even in this respect caution must be exercised since the mute 'e' is one of the common ingredients of traditional French prosody and frequency of use is not in itself an indication that the traditional metre is being undermined; its use must be attended by some ambiguity or some doubt as to its actual value—whether to count it or not—before it can be said to play a part in the dislocation of the form in which it occurs) and then in respect of the 'correspondence' that can be established between the rhythm and the mood of the poem. In the instances of its use in *Romances sans paroles* it is tempting to conclude that Verlaine was striving above all after expressive effects. In fact, its use is in no way outstanding nor in any way novel.

A rhythmic feature of possibly greater importance can be found in the very high percentage of run-on lines. In poems of short lines of four, five or six syllables (e.g. 'Ariette oubliée' viii (p. 55), 'Walcourt' (p. 57) and 'Charleroi' (p. 58)) run-on lines are only to be expected; but their incidence in practically all the other poems is worth noting. Generally speaking they act to break up the regular metric structure by preventing awareness of the syllabic count from becoming too rigidly mechanical. Again, however, too much notice must not be taken of them as an individual feature. They are *one* element in the general tendency Verlaine shows to 'soften' the metric outline. It could be argued, a little perversely perhaps, that Verlaine is notoriously negligent about punctuation; it is going too far to suggest that the large number of run-on lines is due solely to lack of care! Even if that were the case, he is at least consistent in his omission of punctuation at the end of lines. The *Poèmes Saturniens* provide more startling evidence of how far he was prepared to go than do the *Romances sans paroles*. In two poems from the earlier collection, 'Crépuscule du soir mystique' and 'Promenade sentimentale', there is virtually no punctuation at all, each poem containing three end-stopped lines out of thirteen and sixteen lines respectively.

What, only too briefly, the previous paragraphs on rhythm have tried to show is (i) that there is a tendency in *Romances sans paroles* towards what the 'Art poétique' describes as 'plus vague et plus soluble dans l'air' and (ii) that there is nothing revolutionary about the techniques employed. Verlaine remains within a conventional framework even though he prefers to operate in some of its less conventional areas.

Rhyme is really a rhythmical element. Verlaine prefers to treat it separately. It is worth noting that in spite of the injunction of the 'Art poétique':

> Tu feras bien, en train d'énergie,
> De rendre un peu la Rime assagie.
> Si l'on n'y veille, elle ira jusqu'où?
>
> O qui dira les torts de la Rime!
> Quel enfant sourd ou quel nègre fou
> Nous a forgé ce bijou d'un sou
> Qui sonne creux et faux sous la lime?

Verlaine never dispenses with rhyme . . . well, hardly ever. He sees it as an essential part of French prosody. Later, in the 1880s, he would profess a certain scorn for those poets who were to choose to write in free verse. The whole point of Verlaine's little tirade is his impatience with restrictions of too rigid a nature (it would be instructive to know whether Verlaine was familiar with Banville's *Petit Traité de poésie française*, Lemerre, 1871, in which the question of rhyme is developed at great length; it is possible that the section from the 'Art poétique' is Verlaine's answer to, or at least modification of Banville's position; unfortunately there is no means of verifying the suggestion). It is as though he were frightened, or pretending to be, of the possibility that rhyme would tyrannise the whole idea of poetry—or of his own freer idea of what poetry should be ('la chose envolée'). The position rhyme occupies is readily defined: not only is its presence imperative, its use is governed by a single basic rule, as much a matter of actual poetic practice as of legislation—the alternation of masculine and feminine rhyme words; that is, in any rhyme scheme from the most rudimentary *a b b a, a b a b*, etc. to the most complicated, *a* (just as an example) will be masculine and *b* feminine. The system is none the less quite flexible. Most poets accommodate themselves to it without too much apparent difficulty. Verlaine, usually, is no exception. What he does in *Romances sans paroles* is to ignore the rule from time to time. Of the 'Ariettes oubliées', poems ii, iv, viii and ix are written entirely with feminine rhymes. The reason may be sheer impatience with common practice. On the other hand the feminine rhyme word has an extra resonance (because of its mute 'e' ending), a sort of 'dying fall' beyond the sound of the counted syllable which, in its own unobtrusive way, contributes to the attempt to make the line less angular. The particular rhythmic 'softening' is even more noticeable when Verlaine employs run-on lines. The terminal mute 'e' then can take on, if the instance demands it, almost the value of an added syllable. Similar experimentation is continued in the 'Paysages Belges' where the feminine endings of 'Simples Fresques' i (p. 59) are offset by the masculine endings of its companion piece. This is the sort of case in which one is not being too generous to the poet if one says that the feminine rhymes of i are suited to the vagueness of the content and that the clarity of ii is best served by the hardness of the masculine rhymes. In short, the mood of each poem is supported by—and supports—technical decisions of a simple but fundamental nature. There are other examples of a similar sort: the brittleness and apparent cynicism of 'Streets' i (p. 66), the invective and sarcasm of 'Child Wife' (p. 67) seem appropriate to their masculine rhymes. Is it in order to highlight the freedom with which he treats some of the rhyme schemes that Verlaine, in the two poems in the collection written entirely in alexandrines, 'Green' (p. 65) and 'Beams' (p. 69), reverts to conventional treatment? And the whimsy of 'Ariette oubliée' vi is no doubt helped by the lack of rhymes (p. 54).

Again, as is often the case, the experimentation with rhymes requires a wider context than the *Romances sans paroles* by themselves. What Verlaine does in *Romances sans paroles* he had already done in earlier collections, though not to the same extent. As a first gesture in the direction of freedom 'Nevermore' (*Poèmes Saturniens*) contains entire verses of either feminine or masculine rhymes. From the same source 'Croquis Parisien' and 'Un Dahlia' go as far as anything in *Romances sans paroles*: both are written with masculine rhymes alone. *Fêtes Galantes*, too, has its poem in masculine rhymes—'En Sourdine'—and, as far as it is known, the first poem in only feminine rhymes, 'Mandoline'. In that sort of context, no matter how sketchy it is, the boldness of the rhyme schemes in *Romances sans paroles* is not a matter of originality but rather, as with other purely technical features, of an accumulation of effects within a small number of poems. The impression of innovation derives from the high concentration of irregularities, not from the irregularities themselves. These are already part of Verlaine's poetic technique. Only the 'Ariette oubliée' vi (p. 54) represents any advance in terms of freedom. It also represents the most extreme form of Verlaine's assault on established patterns. It is not repeated. In the same way, *Romances sans paroles* represents the end of a line of development in rhythmic freedom. That too is not repeated.

(ii) *Landscape*

One aspect of *Romances sans paroles* which most commentators note is its 'paysages'. Verlaine's 'paysages' tend to be accorded special treatment on account of one outstanding characteristic—the identification of the poet's *état d'âme* with the picture the poet has created. Implied is the disappearance of description for its own sake; the verlainian 'paysage' exists solely as both vehicle for and expression of the poet's mood. It is held to have virtually no meaning as descriptive poetry (whatever that may mean). This view, prevalent though it is, is untenable if it is intended to suggest that Verlaine's poetry operates in a fundamentally different way from that of any other poet. That is not at all to deny the special quality of the verlainian mood nor is it to detract from his personal preferences in terms of vocabulary, subject-matter and so on, nor from his individual way of handling his material; his tone remains quite distinct. Yet even the most objective poetry, the most detailed and 'realistic' descriptions of Leconte de Lisle and Heredia (one could throw in Gautier for good measure), has relatively small value as a form of pure word picture. The most detailed of poems generally leaves quite a margin for the reader's imagination. Not only that, the mood of detached serenity, aloofness, 'impassibilité'—call it by any name that is available—is no less real a mood than one of anxiety, perplexity, distress or melancholy. Each is as much the expression of a personal preference (reinforced in some cases by a poetic theory) as the other; each is reflected in and colours the poetry. And it is perfectly legitimate to state that the mood of

Leconte de Lisle's 'Le Sommeil du Condor' is as much an expression of an *état d'âme* as is 'Il pleure dans mon cœur'. Only it may appear to be less so because the poet, identified by use of the first person singular, chooses to remain absent. In Verlaine's case, however, the one pre-eminent characteristic of the 'paysage' is the way in which the 'je' of the poem transfers its moods to its surroundings, the way in which it *explicitly* states that the *mood* is the most important aspect of the poem, the way in which it implies that the descriptive elements, be they precise or be they representationally vague, are there in order to create the mood rather than present a picture (though they may indeed present a picture as well). Once more, though, the examples of this which occur in *Romances sans paroles* are neither new nor unexpected. They represent the culmination of a style of writing which has its beginnings in the *Poèmes Saturniens* and the persistence of which Verlaine recognised in his 'Critique des *Poèmes Saturniens*' (written in January 1890 and published on 15 March 1890 in *La Revue d'aujourd'hui* to coincide with a re-edition of the *Poèmes Saturniens*): 'mais plus on me lira, plus on se convaincra qu'une sorte d'unité relie mes choses premières à celles de mon âge mûr: par exemple les *Paysages tristes* ne sont-ils pas en quelque sorte l'œuf de toute une volée de vers chanteurs, vagues ensemble et définis, dont je suis peut-être le premier en date oiselier? On l'a imprimé du moins' ('Prose', p. 721). Setting aside the claim to originality, which may well be justified with regard to the *Poèmes Saturniens* but which cannot be gone into here, there remains the important, and deliberate, assertion that the poems in the 'Paysages tristes'—seven in all—are related, or can be related to similar poems in later collections. With one exception, 'L'Heure du Berger', the poems establish perfectly clearly the link between the poet and the 'paysage':

> Mon cœur qui s'oublie
> Aux soleils couchants.
> ('Soleils Couchants')

> Moi j'errais tout seul, promenant ma plaie
> Au long de l'étang
> ('Promenade sentimentale')

Comme un vol criard d'oiseaux en émoi,
Tous mes souvenirs s'abattent sur moi
('Le Rossignol')

—and so on; there are quite a number of examples. The link between the poet and the landscape is not made in an identical manner each time, but there can be no doubt that it is made and that the reader is thereby openly invited to see the 'paysage' in terms of it being a representation of the poet's mood. Verlaine does, perhaps more obviously, what any poet does: he achieves two things for the price of one—a description and a personal mood. In other words the language he uses operates on a fairly literal level (though not a *realist* level) at the same time as on a figurative level. In his 'Paysages tristes' Verlaine makes it totally certain that both levels are heeded. He proceeds in a similar manner in subsequent collections. In *Fêtes Galantes*, for instance, 'Clair de lune' begins: 'Votre âme est un paysage choisi' (the substitution of 'vous' for 'moi' might tend to take the reader away from the poet's own mood, but it in no way alters the mechanics of the method) and 'En Sourdine' is full of this particular type of 'mingling':

Fondons nos âmes, nos cœurs
Et nos sens extasiés,
Parmi les vagues langueurs
Des pins et des arbousiers.

Even *La Bonne Chanson* can be seen to remain faithful, in part, to the pattern, especially in

La lune blanche
Luit dans les bois

where the personal intrusion, for being most discreetly done, and for including not only the poet but also his companion—a favourite device—is no less real. In the light, therefore, of examples of this sort the practice of the 'paysages' in *Romances sans paroles*, while doubtless unique in its particular flavour—though even then likenesses can be traced back to such poems as 'Soleils couchants', 'Chanson d'Automne', 'A Clymène' and 'La lune blanche'—is not a manifestation of a new approach. In the 'Ariettes oubliées' the poet and the 'paysage' continue to receive separate mention—of a very subtle sort in 'Dans l'interminable Ennui' where the poet's presence is suggested and not openly stated—and the poet's apparent intention is still to mingle the 'paysage' and the personal mood by drawing attention to the fact even if, as in the first and fifth 'Ariette', he does so by asking a question rather than by making a statement. Nothing in fact could sum up the position more clearly than the second verse of 'Ariette oubliée' ix:

Combien, ô voyageur, ce paysage blême
  Te mira blême toi-même,
Et que tristes pleuraient dans les hautes feuillées
  Tes espérances noyées!

In a sense, then, the poet is not a disinterested spectator but an emotionally involved participant. How this type of involvement in the 'paysage' is interpreted is, however, an entirely different matter and depends a great deal on personal opinion and emphasis. It has been suggested, quite plausibly, that Verlaine is attempting to lose his personality in the landscape. Indeed, that may be as good a way as any of expressing the peculiar sort of osmosis which these poems convey, but the obvious reason for supposing such a desire on the poet's part is the evidence of the words themselves. No matter what way it is described or elaborated on, the essential point remains unaltered: the 'paysage' exists principally as a vehicle for the poet's mood. Verlaine goes to some length to make that particular point abundantly clear.

What is not clear, so to speak, is the imagery, the 'paysages' themselves. Again, it is customary to come up against ideas about 'suggestion', 'impressionism', Verlaine's 'sensibilité' or his acute visual perception. No doubt such ideas are appropriate and accurate enough. Verlaine's own term is simply 'vagues' (to which he adds 'définis', an odd combination of qualities). And that, if one may be equally simple about it, is exactly what the 'paysages' are. Verlaine gives enough information to allow a picture of sorts to form in the reader's imagination, but the picture so formed is remarkably hazy in terms of its relationship to what one normally sees. Most of the 'impressionistic' poems contain only few *visible* objects. Those which do contain a relatively large proportion, 'Ariettes oubliées' v (p. 53) and viii (p. 55), 'Walcourt' (p. 57) and so on, never allow a realistic picture to emerge because the detail is presented either unadorned, as in 'Walcourt', and is therefore of a general, non-specific sort, or it is qualified in a manner which fuzzes the outline. On close analysis most of Verlaine's 'pictures' are less than rudimentary. In addition, Verlaine uses large numbers of abstract nouns or nouns which carry no visual association ('Ariette oubliée' i is full of them—'extase', 'fatigue', 'frissons', 'voix', 'murmure', 'plainte', 'soir' etc.) and which, in any case, are drawn from such common and widely used areas as to have no really precise definition except in terms of the way they function within a given context. When these words themselves form the greater part of the context then the poem remains, and must indeed remain, vague. A useful example is the 'Ariette oubliée' iii (p. 52) where the concrete nouns are 'ville', 'pluie', 'terre' and 'toits' ('cœur' is not being offered as a precise anatomical image!). These sign-words—for such they are, empty frames for the reader to see whatever town/roofs/earth he so chooses—are given the most imprecise of visual contexts: 'Il pleure . . . il pleut . . . langueur . . . bruit doux . . . s'ennuie . . . chant . . . raison . . . trahison . . . deuil . . . peine . . . amour . . . haine'. At best, what Verlaine builds is a mood with what might be called pictorial adjuncts; no amount of juggling with what Verlaine offers could ever produce a *picture* without a substantial contribution from the reader himself. The *mood*, on the other hand, is much less dependent on the readers' imagination. Like the 'picture' it is vague, fleeting and curiously ill-defined— except in Verlaine's own definition of it. If the mood were to be characterised then, roughly, it could be deemed 'sad'. Having said as much, any further definition has necessarily to be on Verlaine's terms or on none at all, since any re-definition in words other than those used in the poem is a falsification of what is actually there even though it may go under the laudable name of 'explanation' or 'interpretation'. In short, Verlaine's 'vague' is as close as one can get to a definition of the 'paysage' without distorting it and without attaching any further labels to it.

To determine what is 'défini' about the 'paysages' is a much more tricky operation. Verlaine gives no help whatsoever. It would seem, however, that there are three not unreasonable ways of suggesting what might be meant by 'défini'. Firstly, it could be argued that the poems are autobiographical in nature (in a general sense) and relate more or less directly to Verlaine's mood at a given time. In that way they are a 'definite' indication concerning the state of mind of the poet. It is not an explanation that carries much conviction. Secondly it may be that because the mood is confined to a narrow band at the sad/melancholic end of the spectrum, then the 'definition' relates to the fact that the overall tone is very limited. Again, the explanation is no more than a possibility. Finally it may be that the idea of 'definition' is not a question of mood at all, but a question of syntax and structure, because in the verlainian 'paysage' there is no grammatical or structural vagueness; the vague content is put across in a clear and quite logical manner. The vagueness derives from the choice of words as such, and not from their putting together in the poem. Verlaine always seems to prefer a simple syntactical framework. Therein may (or may not) lie the answer to the idea that Verlaine's 'paysages', for all their nebulous qualities, contain an element which Verlaine himself chose to describe as 'défini'. (See commentaries on the 'Ariettes oubliées', pp. 71–85).

The last point is the one connected with the idea of 'vers chanteurs', an idea which has assumed considerable importance with regard to Verlaine's poetry. What is at issue is the question of musical poetry. Philosophical and aesthetic theories apart, musicality in poetry derives from two main sources: imagery and sound-pattern. To be brief, as far as the former is concerned the more 'musical' an image is, the more it is representationally indefinite (i.e. vague). In view of what has just been said about Verlaine's vagueness, all that need be added is that the 'Ariettes oubliées' can be considered the most musical section of the *Romances sans paroles*, always assuming it can be agreed that it is legitimate to talk about 'musical' imagery where representational indefiniteness is concerned. But one suspects it was the latter that was uppermost in Verlaine's mind when he wrote of 'vers chanteurs'. Sound-pattern, in fact, is generally thought of as the most outstanding 'musical' feature of Verlaine's poetry. Taking the 'Paysages tristes' as a starting point it is evident that a large percentage of them conform to the description, albeit vague, of 'vers chanteurs', notably 'Soleils couchants', 'Promenade sentimentale' and 'Chanson d'Automne'. In the first and last mentioned poems the sound-effects depend to a large extent on the predominance of the rhyme words in the short lines and in addition, in 'Soleils couchants', on the repetition of various words or even complete lines—with minor variations to suit the syntax. 'Promenade sentimentale' depends much less on the rhyme words and much more on the repetition of phrases and images, though always—and the point is important—with indistinct images. Without going into detail, a lot of the effect of these poems comes from their highly patterned structure which, on one level at least, is a sound structure.

The sound-patterns of *Romances sans paroles* are made up of similar elements (though perhaps less mechanistic in their application). Fundamentally it is a question of seeing that one or more sorts of repetition—single sounds, whole words, groups of words or even closely related ideas—are used in a way which suggests that the recurrence of certain groups of sounds is a deliberate feature of Verlaine's style. Not that the sound-pattern can be taken without reference to the meaning. In fact it could be maintained that the sound-pattern becomes an element of the meaning, reinforcing in a non-discursive way, the logical, rational structure of the poems. From this point of view repetition is 'musical' because it highlights the tonal side of the poem by drawing attention to what might rightly be called the *flesh* of the words. To some extent, of course, this is what happens in all traditional French poetry simply because there is a regular syllable count and a rhyme word. But such a basic sound-pattern is, for Verlaine, only a framework on which to hang all manner of variations. Whereas traditional sound-patterns are, by their very nature and position within the verse, regular, the most noticeable feature of Verlaine's variations is that they are *irregular*. They tend to occur at unequal intervals. Therein lies a considerable amount of their charm. The regular, metrical sound-pattern of the rhyme is, as it were, set off by a number of much freer patterns. The result is a form of tonal tension, a form of structural tightening which goes some way towards providing a 'corrective' to the evanescent quality of the imagery. At the same time, the sound-patterns serve to emphasise the vagueness of the meaning in so far as they direct attention away from what is being said to how it is being said. Sound-patterns, therefore, can be considered as having a dual function. Given the vagueness of much of *Romances sans paroles* their function in terms of structural tightening might be regarded as something of a necessity.

This 'musical' side of Verlaine's poetry has drawn considerable comment, beginning with Blémont's efforts on the appearance of *Romances sans paroles* (see p. 2). Most of the comment is imprecise and couched in the sort of language that does no more than skid across the surface of the problem. André Barre, in his thesis *Le Symbolisme* (Jouve et Cie, 1911), writes: 'quoi de moins explicable, mais aussi quoi de plus charmeur que ces *Romances sans paroles*, . . . où le vers semble n'être que la forme écrite de la mélodie. La poésie de Verlaine est pour ainsi dire la musique même; elle se sent, elle ne s'analyse pas' (pp. 185–6). Or again, François Porché (*Verlaine tel qu'il fut*, p. 171) can say: '*Romances sans paroles* marque l'intention de tirer une musique des mots, abstraction faite de leur contenu intellectuel'. Such an opinion is no more than a fairly obvious gloss on the title itself. What comments of this nature do is draw attention to the so-called 'musical' facet of Verlaine's poetry without really making any attempt to find out what it consists of, nor indeed to query the necessity for using the word 'musical'. Because, as to the word itself, while it may be possible to justify its use figuratively (there can be no *literal* justification), it achieved its currency mainly through Verlaine's efforts to provide himself with some sort of publicity. The success of the idea of 'musical' poetry was largely due to the generation of poets following Verlaine (Kahn and Merrill, for example) but it led them to a conception of poetry which did both poetry and Verlaine a disservice; just as it has led a fair number of critics to exaggerate the value of this side of Verlaine's poetry. Nadal's summing up of the position is to date the most accurate (provided one takes the word 'musique' with a certain amount of scepticism): 'C'est par la musique plus que par l'image que Verlaine fit perdre au langage sa vertu commune de représentation [the proposition could be queried]. Encore n'a-t-il pas détruit l'accord ou la connivence secrète de ce que les mots disent et de leur chant; mais il en a exténué le sens, en attribuant aux formes sensibles et originelles de la voix un rôle prépondérant' (pp. 88–9)[7].

Once more, however, it is difficult to avoid the conclusion that the 'musicality' of Verlaine's *Romances sans paroles* is not a new feature but a continuation of trends begun in the *Poèmes Saturniens*, just as it might conceivably be argued that the much more 'precise' descriptions of parts of the 'Paysages Belges' and 'Aquarelles' were foreshadowed by the 'Eaux-fortes' of the same earlier collection and that the anecdotal poetry of 'Birds in the Night' exists in large measure in *La Bonne Chanson*. Such an observation does nothing to diminish the excellence of much of the poetry in *Romances sans paroles*. It does raise an interesting query concerning the evolution of Verlaine's poetry after 1874 given the fact (if such it is) that in many respects *Romances sans paroles* represents the culmination of certain trends in Verlaine's poetic development. To have continued to develop along similar lines would probably (the point is hypothetical but seems worth making) have had more than one undesirable effect on Verlaine's poetry; undesirable, that is, in his own eyes in the first instance. On the technical side it could have meant the eventual abandonment of traditional forms. Verlaine was never able to go so far. Indeed, he was to see no real justification for free verse and argued that the traditional prosody ought to be retained; see, for example, *Epigrammes* ii where he is prepared to admit his own role in the process of freeing traditional metre from too stultifying a stiffness but where he still considers metre and rhyme as indispensable to what he calls 'notre art français'. On the 'impressionistic' side it could have meant becoming increasingly vague and running the risk of losing all comprehensibility. On the 'musical' side it could have led to an excessive use of repetitive devices and to concentration on sound for sound's sake. Worst of all would have been the almost unavoidable risk of self-parody. One might regret that henceforth Verlaine's poems were, generally speaking, less technically experimental and more specifically anecdotal or representational; but one should not lose sight of the fact that a certain verlainian vein, in *Romances sans paroles*, has been exploited to the full and has produced a remarkably rich yield, in quality if not in quantity.

(iii) *The Expression of Feelings*

By the time the ever astute Léon Vanier came to publish the second edition of *Romances sans paroles* in 1887 Verlaine's reputation was firmly established. *Sagesse*, dated 1881, came out in December 1880 (Vanier produced a second edition in 1889) and *Jadis et Naguère* in 1884 (again, Vanier had a second edition on the market in 1891). It is instructive to note that the first editions of *Romances sans paroles*, *Sagesse* and *Jadis et Naguère* were limited to 300, 500 and 500 copies respectively, whereas the second editions were of 600, 1,100 and 1,100 copies. If nothing else, the figures suggest an increase in Verlaine's popularity—and Vanier's exploitation of it. The 'Art poétique' had been published in 1882 and amply commented on. In addition the weekly periodical *Lutèce* began publishing the first of the set of articles known as *Les Poètes maudits* in its issue of 29 March–5 April 1884. At the end of the same year Vanier brought out the essays on Corbière, Rimbaud and Mallarmé in a small volume. Three more essays followed, on Marceline Desbordes-Valmore, Villiers de L'Isle-Adam and Verlaine himself (Pauvre Lélian). It was Vanier who published the six in one volume in 1888. If that were not enough, the *Mémoires d'un veuf* saw the light of day in 1886, as too did the short stories *Louise Leclercq*, etc. Verlaine had also begun to write his contributions to the series *Les Hommes d'aujourd'hui*. Public recognition (of sorts) was confirmed when Huysmans published *A Rebours* in 1884. Drawing the reader's attention to the delights of a number of contemporary literary figures, Huysmans included Verlaine. His pioneering appreciation of some of the qualities in Verlaine's poetry was to prove as representative of a particular way of approaching Verlaine's poetry as anything that was to be written in the following fifty or so years: 'Mais sa personnalité résidait surtout en ceci: qu'il avait pu exprimer de vagues et délicieuses confidences, à mi-voix, au crépuscule. Seul, il avait pu laisser deviner certains au-delà troublants d'âme, des chuchotements si bas de pensées, des aveux si murmurés, si interrompus, que l'oreille qui les percevait, demeurait hésitante, coulant à l'âme des langueurs avivées par le mystère de ce souffle plus deviné que senti' (Chapter 14). It is this question of mood, tone, atmosphere, sensation—call it what you will—that dominates most critical appreciations of Verlaine from the 1880s onwards. In his short but very sympathetic *Paul Verlaine* Charles Morice is without hesitation on this point: *Romances sans paroles* is at the beginning of it, 'c'est d'elles que date . . . cet art suggestif, ce nouveau monde où les nouveaux artistes se cherchent des royaumes . . . merveilles de pures sensations et de correspondances . . .' (pp. 34–6). Similarly, in the funeral oration that François Coppée delivered in 1896, there is great emphasis on the same sort of qualities; Verlaine's poetry is described as 'naïve et subtile . . . évocatrice des plus délicates vibrations des nerfs, des plus fugitifs échos du cœur . . . harmonie délicieuse . . . déjà de la musique . . . [Verlaine] nous a montré son âme si troublée mais si ingénue' (this oration serves as a preface to *Paul Verlaine, Choix de Poésies*, Charpentier, 1936). It seems quite clear that as early as 1896, earlier even, certain lines of approach have been irrevocably laid down. Coppée is simply articulating the commonly held view of Verlaine's poetry. It is a view which is applied more and more to one collection: *Romances sans paroles*, a collection 'où vibre intense la vie dans sa nudité douloureuse' (Achille Delaroche in the commemorative number of *La Plume*, February 1896, p. 81), a collection full of 'l'*ineffable* de nos sentiments modernes; cela en une forme délicieusement adéquate, lumineuse, diaphane et chantante, contournée et mélancolique et douce . . .' (Henri Van de Putte in the same number, pp. 105–6). The opinion even spreads across the Channel. Arthur Symons in *The Symbolist Movement in Literature* (Heinemann, 1899) writes convincingly of Verlaine's 'susceptibility of the senses' (revised edition of 1919, p. 47). This view of Verlaine receives official confirmation in André Barre's *Le Symbolisme*. A full forty pages are devoted to the poet. They abound with comments such as: 'L'essentiel, c'est d'abréger la distance entre la sensation et l'expression . . . il faut donner du jour au vers, de l'air à la phrase, assouplir, amollir, fluidifier la cire expressive du langage pour la contraindre à mouler toutes les arabesques de la sensation et de la pensée'. Quotations of a similar nature could be taken from virtually any critic, including the most recent. J.-P. Richard, for example, in *Poésie et Profondeur* even goes so far as to assert that Verlaine's originality 'était toute entière située sur le plan du sentir' (pp. 184–5). In short, Verlaine's poetry was, and apparently still is, held to 'traduire des sensations'. What is meant by that is, presumably, something to do with the poetry being primarily *immediately affective*. But it cannot be that alone; almost any poem is immediately affective to a greater or lesser extent. Baudelaire's

> O toison, moutonnant jusque sur l'encolure!
> O boucles! O parfum chargé de nonchaloir!
> Extase! . . .

is not lacking in 'sensations', even though the various 'sensations' are operative in an emotive/philosophical context which is very different from Verlaine's, but the 'sensations', to put it crudely, are being used as means to an end and not, as it were, *for their own sake*. It is the use of 'sensations' for their own sake which, it is suggested, is the peculiarity of Verlaine's poetry. It is not that Verlaine's poetry outdoes that of other poets in the expression of sensations, it is that it does nothing else. The poems do not reach out beyond themselves to imply some system of extra-poetic values; they do not lend themselves to interpretations of an ethical or philosophical nature; there is no deeper meaning, no symbolism. The prime examples of this sort of poetry are the 'Ariettes oubliées'. They represent the limits of this 'poetry of sensation'. That is why 'C'est l'extase langoureuse' and 'Je devine à travers un murmure' are difficult to interpret in terms of outside references. They lack a framework into which they can be conveniently put. Therefore, if they are to represent anything at all, what they do represent ('express' would be a better word) are fleeting moments of feeling, small eddies on the surface of existence, evanescent moods which come and go at whim. That is all. There are no lessons to be learnt, no conclusions to be drawn. One's appreciation of this side of Verlaine's art could, in fact, stop there. Yet it is quite evident that for many commentators (and readers, no doubt) a view which is content to see the 'Ariettes oubliées' solely in terms of the expression of evanescent feelings is considered unsatisfactory and ultimately inadequate.

Verlaine's ability to express feeling is not at stake. What is put forward is the view that because Verlaine is able to express such feelings so accurately, or at least so convincingly; because his apparent knowledge of them is so extensive and so intimate, then what he is actually doing is expressing his *own* experience of those feelings. That particular approach was the first to be generally adopted. Retté puts it clearly enough in his article in *La Plume* of February 1896: 'comment oublier l'homme en lui puisque sa poésie n'était que le commentaire de tout son être' (p. 118). He even goes so far as to assert that Verlaine had no choice but to express his own feelings: 'mais inconscient et magnifique ainsi qu'une force naturelle, il chantait ses vers *parce qu'il ne pouvait pas faire autrement*. "Je sens donc je suis" telle eût pu être sa devise' (ibid., p. 116). Regardless of how blatantly or of how cleverly the view is put—and the variations are enormous—the basic position remains constant. In a sense it cannot be disputed. Verlaine lends it his own authority in both the correspondence and the critical articles where, to take only one example, from his 'Conférence sur les poètes contemporains' ('Prose', p. 901), he writes, 'mais du regret et du dépit, puis quelques consolations, compensations plutôt, l'inspirèrent [talking of himself] dans son troisième [*sic*] recueil: *Romances sans paroles*'. Yet, really, that particular knowledge adds nothing to the poetry that is not, in some measure, already taken for granted—that whatever Verlaine writes about has some definite relation to what can be called his own subjectivity; that what he writes must be coloured by the way he experiences events, even though it is impossible to determine the exact degree of relationship between an 'event' and the poet's expression of it. To say Verlaine is expressing his own feelings is to beg too many questions, no matter how obvious that conclusion seems.

A more plausible, and possibly more acceptable, variation of this sort of approach consists in examining extensively the *state of mind* that the poems as a whole are said to exhibit. The most highly developed of these approaches are those of Nadal, Richard and Borel. Richard develops his argument along lines of passive receptivity linked with the central idea of the 'pur sentir'. Nadal and Borel pursue the idea of the poetry being connected with a dream-like state of mind. In Nadal's case the argument (which is persuasively presented) depends on establishing the primacy of 'la vie du songe'. 'Pour Verlaine', he writes, 'ce *songe* est *vérité* . . . il choisit le songe comme l'unique refuge, *la région où vivre*' (pp. 18–19). However, the Verlainian dream is not some-thing that excludes the outside world; on the contrary, the world is absorbed into the dream to become 'le milieu même de l'esprit qui le songe' (p. 26). 'Les images ne s'y déroulent plus comme sur une toile; elles constituent le lieu dont la rêverie prend possession comme de son domaine' (ibid.). In *Romances sans paroles*, at least in the 'Ariettes oubliées', the identity of the real world and the poet's inner world is seen as total, and since the real world is presented as 'un monde en perpétuel déséquilibre et effacement', then that is the direct result of the poet's state of mind, 'une conscience rêveuse qui n'a plus de point fixe, de références, d'identité' (p. 15). Here again the question of 'sen-sations' turns out to be of great importance: 'Verlaine infléchit la rêverie vers une désappropriation de plus en plus marquée des facultés intellectuelles et volontaires—raison, logique, désir, souvenir—et nous donne comme le voulait Rimbaud une *traduction immédiate du senti*' (p. 53). Nadal adds the not negligeable rider to the effect that even when Verlaine's dreamlike state is at its most pronounced, 'la subjectivité, témoignages et anecdotes person-nelles, colle à ses poèmes même les plus visionnaires' (p. 63). It could indeed be argued that anecdote colours all of 'Birds in the Night' and a large part of both the 'Paysages Belges' and the 'Aquarelles'.

Borel's position reinforces Nadal's but goes even further, claiming that Verlaine's poetry reveals a man 'devant sa propre rêverie' and given over to 'l'effarement d'un être en proie au songe' ('Poésie', p. 12). *Romances sans paroles* is evidence of 'un vertigineux affolement' (p. 21), but contains enough anecdotal material to show that Verlaine was frightened by what the 'Ariettes oubliées' revealed of his true nature and that he preferred, possibly for sanity's sake, to return to the less demand-ing paths and safer ways of 'Birds in the Night'.

This type of interpretation may not be to everyone's taste, but it has the advantage of concentrating on the poems rather than on the poet (though it may draw conclusions regarding the poet). It seeks to establish a dominant principle behind the poems and then relate that principle to what it sees as a permanent feature of the poet's psychological make-up. Whether the eventual link with the poet is justified is another matter.

Poetry is not altogether a trustworthy medium. However, the approach does mean that a lot is learned about the poetry (the three critics mentioned are never less than interesting and are often quite enviably illuminating) and that a certain amount is learned, or at least assumed, about the poet.

There is still another means of approach—perhaps the most obvious and in some respects the most understandable. It consists in drawing very close parallels between Verlaine's life and his poetry, and it can still be justified by being related to the business of expressing feelings: if Verlaine is able to express feelings so accurately, it follows that they are his own feelings, not of a general nature but specifically related to the observable events of his life. There can be no question that Verlaine's poetry does lend itself with extraordinary facility to what is a straightforward autobiographical interpretation. To take only the minimum of examples—*La Bonne Chanson* is the direct outcome of his engagement to Mathilde; *Sagesse* expresses his (re)conversion to the Catholic faith; a substantial part of *Amour* is devoted to Verlaine's feelings towards Lucien Létinois and the *Chansons pour Elle* are a fairly direct rendering (in some respects) of his relationship with Eugénie Krantz. 'No poet's work is more intimately bound up with his life than Paul Verlaine's' (A. E. Carter in *Verlaine: a study in parallels*, p. vii). On that basic assumption, what more natural than to state that *Romances sans paroles* 'reflects his troubled emotional state over the rupture with his wife and his liaison with Rimbaud' (Perman, *Verlaine—Selected Poems*, p. 13); that the same volume is 'l'écho du conflit des années 1871–3 entre deux amours et deux mondes' (Zimmermann, p. 56); that the poems in it 'ne s'expliquent bien que par les circonstances où elles furent composées' (Adam, p. 92). The general parallel, even when it is stated as explicitly as this, is by and large acceptable, because all it says is that the poet writes out of his own experience. But the case does not stop there. If *Romances sans paroles* as a whole derives from a specific period in Verlaine's life, then it follows that the individual poems should be traceable to specific events within that period. Initially the four sections of the volume are placed according to their 'inspiration'—'Ariettes oubliées' and 'Aquarelles' are divided between Mathilde and Rimbaud; 'Birds in the Night' are placed

under Mathilde's star and the 'Paysages Belges' under
Rimbaud's. From there each individual poem receives its
appointed designation. It is precisely at this point that problems
arise, especially over the attribution of the 'Ariettes oubliées'. Is
'Ariette oubliée' iv: 'Il faut, voyez-vous . . .' about Mathilde or
Rimbaud? What of 'C'est l'extase langoureuse', or 'Il pleure
dans mon cœur'? And is it really demonstrable that in
'Aquarelles' 'les poèmes à Mathilde et à Rimbaud alternent'
(Zimmermann, p. 57)? A certain scepticism must be allowed
regarding claims of that nature, even though there is no reason
to doubt the *sources* of Verlaine's inspiration (though again, in
general terms). The sources are not in dispute. Nor is the fact
that the poems have to do with Verlaine's relationship with
Mathilde and Rimbaud. What is at issue is the relevance of
saying that the fifth 'Ariette oubliée' is 'about' the 'petit boudoir
de la rue Nicolet où flotte encore son [Mathilde's] parfum' and
the 'petit jardin qui sépare la maison de la chaussée' or that the
eighth 's'explique par le voyage que Verlaine fit à Paliseul à la
fin de décembre 1871' and that the third may have been written
in London in October 1872 (see Adam, pp. 93–4). If such excur-
sions into the poet's daily activities have any point at all, then
they are connected with the business of establishing the possible
time and place of composition of certain poems; only on a most
superficial level can they be considered explanations of the
poems. It may be reassuring to think that as a result of walking
in the snow at Paliseul Verlaine wrote:

> La neige incertaine
> Luit comme du sable

but it cannot be maintained, except perversely, that

> Dans l'interminable
> Ennui

is essentially, if indeed at all, about a walk in the snow. The
poem is not versified autobiography. At best the background
events of the poet's life may make it easier to understand why he
wrote certain types of poems, but autobiography is a terribly
crude and blunt instrument with which to dissect such fragile
creations as the 'Ariettes oubliées'. In the last resort it is ir-

relevant whether the mood expressed in a certain poem was the mood as Verlaine actually experienced it. What matters is his ability to make the reader live it. Cluttering the reader's approach with psychological insights, with titillating revelations about the poet's moral misdemeanours is much more likely to pre-determine the reader's response in the wrong way than to provide any genuine literary criteria with which to judge the poems. If there is to be any pre-judging it might be better to leave it to Verlaine himself who said that *Romances sans paroles* was given that title 'pour mieux exprimer le vrai vague et le manque de sens précis projetés'.

Ariettes oubliées

i

Le vent dans la plaine
Suspend son haleine.
Favart

C'est l'extase langoureuse,
C'est la fatigue amoureuse,
C'est tous les frissons des bois   3
Parmi l'étreinte des brises,
C'est, vers les ramures grises,
Le chœur des petites voix.   6

O le frêle et frais murmure !
Cela gazouille et susurre,
Cela ressemble au cri doux   9
Que l'herbe agitée expire . . .
Tu dirais, sous l'eau qui vire,
Le roulis sourd des cailloux.   1 2

Cette âme qui se lamente
En cette plainte dormante,
C'est la nôtre, n'est-ce pas ?   1 5
La mienne, dis, et la tienne,
Dont s'exhale l'humble antienne
Par ce tiède soir, tout bas ?   1 8

ii

Je devine, à travers un murmure,
Le contour subtil des voix anciennes
Et dans les lueurs musiciennes,
Amour pâle, une aurore future !   4

Et mon âme et mon cœur en délires
Ne sont plus qu'une espèce d'œil double
Où tremblote à travers un jour trouble
L'ariette, hélas! de toutes lyres!   8

O mourir de cette mort seulette
Que s'en vont, cher amour qui t'épeures,
Balançant jeunes et vieilles heures!
O mourir de cette escarpolette!   12

iii

Il pleut doucement sur la ville.
Arthur Rimbaud

Il pleure dans mon cœur
Comme il pleut sur la ville,
Quelle est cette langueur
Qui pénètre mon cœur?   4

O bruit doux de la pluie
Par terre et sur les toits!
Pour un cœur qui s'ennuie
O le chant de la pluie!   8

Il pleure sans raison
Dans ce cœur qui s'écœure.
Quoi! nulle trahison?
Ce deuil est sans raison.   12

C'est bien la pire peine
De ne savoir pourquoi,
Sans amour et sans haine,
Mon cœur a tant de peine!   16

iv

Il faut, voyez-vous, nous pardonner les choses.
De cette façon nous serons bien heureuses,
Et si notre vie a des instants moroses,
Du moins nous serons, n'est-ce pas? deux pleureuses.   4

O que nous mêlions, âmes sœurs que nous sommes,
A nos vœux confus la douceur puérile
De cheminer loin des femmes et des hommes,
Dans le frais oubli de ce qui nous exile!   8

Soyons deux enfants, soyons deux jeunes filles
Eprises de rien et de tout étonnées,
Qui s'en vont pâlir sous les chastes charmilles
Sans même savoir qu'elles sont pardonnées.   12

v

Son joyeux, importun, d'un clavecin sonore.
                    Pétrus Borel

Le piano que baise une main frêle
Luit dans le soir rose et gris vaguement,
Tandis qu'avec un très léger bruit d'aile   3
Un air bien vieux, bien faible et bien charmant
Rôde discret, épeuré quasiment,
Par le boudoir longtemps parfumé d'Elle.   6

Qu'est-ce que c'est que ce berceau soudain
Qui lentement dorlote mon pauvre être?
Que voudrais-tu de moi, doux chant badin?   9
Qu'as-tu voulu, fin refrain incertain
Qui vas tantôt mourir vers la fenêtre
Ouverte un peu sur le petit jardin?   12

vi

C'est le chien de Jean de Nivelle
Qui mord sous l'œil même du guet
Le chat de la mère Michel;
François-les-bas-bleus s'en égaie.   4

La lune à l'écrivain public
Dispense sa lumière obscure
Où Médor avec Angélique
Verdissent sur le pauvre mur.   8

Et voici venir La Ramée
Sacrant en bon soldat du Roi.
Sous son habit blanc mal famé,
Son cœur ne se tient pas de joie,   12

Car la boulangère . . . —Elle?—Oui dam!
Bernant Lustucru, son vieil homme,
A tantôt couronné sa flamme . . .
Enfants, *Dominus vobis-cum*!   16

Place! en sa longue robe bleue
Toute en satin qui fait frou-frou,
C'est une impure, palsambleu!
Dans sa chaise qu'il faut qu'on loue,   20

Fût-on philosophe ou grigou,
Car tant d'or s'y relève en bosse,
Que ce luxe insolent bafoue
Tout le papier de monsieur Loss!   24

Arrière, robin crotté! place,
Petit courtaud, petit abbé,
Petit poète jamais las
De la rime non attrapée!   28

Voici que la nuit vraie arrive . . .
Cependant jamais fatigué
D'être inattentif et naïf
François-les-bas-bleus s'en égaie.   32

vii

O triste, triste était mon âme
A cause, à cause d'une femme.

Je ne me suis pas consolé
Bien que mon cœur s'en soit allé,   4

Bien que mon cœur, bien que mon âme
Eussent fui loin de cette femme.

Je ne me suis pas consolé,
Bien que mon cœur s'en soit allé.   8

Et mon cœur, mon cœur trop sensible
Dit à mon âme: Est-il possible,

Est-il possible, —le fût-il, —
Ce fier exil, ce triste exil?   12

Mon âme dit à mon cœur: Sais-je
Moi-même, que nous veut ce piège

D'être présents bien qu'exilés,
Encore que loin en allés?   16

viii

Dans l'interminable
Ennui de la plaine
La neige incertaine
Luit comme du sable.   4

Le ciel est de cuivre
Sans lueur aucune.
On croirait voir vivre
Et mourir la lune.   8

Comme des nuées
Flottent gris les chênes
Des forêts prochaines
Parmi les buées.   12

Le ciel est de cuivre
Sans lueur aucune.
On croirait voir vivre
Et mourir la lune.   16

Corneille poussive
Et vous, les loups maigres,
Par ces bises aigres
Quoi donc vous arrive?   20

Dans l'interminable
Ennui de la plaine
La neige incertaine
Luit comme du sable.   24

ix

Le rossignol, qui du haut d'une branche
se regarde dedans, croit être tombé dans
la rivière. Il est au sommet d'un chêne
et toutefois il a peur de se noyer.
Cyrano de Bergerac

L'ombre des arbres dans la rivière embrumée
    Meurt comme de la fumée,
Tandis qu'en l'air, parmi les ramures réelles,
    Se plaignent les tourterelles.   4

Combien, ô voyageur, ce paysage blême
   Te mira blême toi-même,
Et que tristes pleuraient dans les hautes feuillées
   Tes espérances noyées!   8

Mai, juin 1872

Paysages Belges

'Conquestes du Roy'
(Vieilles estampes)

WALCOURT

Briques et tuiles,
O les charmants
Petits asiles
Pour les amants!   4

Houblons et vignes,
Feuilles et fleurs,
Tentes insignes
Des francs buveurs!   8

Guinguettes claires,
Bières, clameurs,
Servantes chères
A tous fumeurs!   12

Gares prochaines,
Gais chemins grands . . .
Quelles aubaines,
Bons juifs errants!   16

Juillet 1872

CHARLEROI

Dans l'herbe noire
Les Kobolds vont.
Le vent profond
Pleure, on veut croire.   4

Quoi donc se sent?
L'avoine siffle.
Un buisson gifle
L'œil au passant.   8

Plutôt des bouges
Que des maisons.
Quels horizons
De forges rouges!   1 2

On sent donc quoi?
Des gares tonnent,
Les yeux s'étonnent,
Où Charleroi?   1 6

Parfums sinistres!
Qu'est-ce que c'est?
Quoi bruissait
Comme des sistres?   20

Sites brutaux!
Oh! votre haleine,
Sueur humaine,
Cris des métaux!   24

Dans l'herbe noire
Les Kobolds vont.
Le vent profond
Pleure, on veut croire.   28

BRUXELLES

Simples Fresques

i

La fuite est verdâtre et rose
Des collines et des rampes,
Dans un demi-jour de lampes
Qui vient brouiller toute chose.   4

L'or, sur les humbles abîmes,
Tout doucement s'ensanglante,
Des petits arbres sans cimes,
Où quelque oiseau faible chante.   8

Triste à peine tant s'effacent
Ces apparences d'automne,
Toutes mes langueurs rêvassent,
Que berce l'air monotone.   12

ii

L'allée est sans fin
Sous le ciel, divin
D'être pâle ainsi!   3
Sais-tu qu'on serait
Bien sous le secret
De ces arbres-ci?   6

Des messieurs bien mis,
Sans nul doute amis
Des Royer-Collards,   9
Vont vers le château.
J'estimerais beau
D'être ces vieillards.   12

Le château, tout blanc
Avec, à son flanc,
Le soleil couché.   15
Les champs à l'entour . . .
Oh! que notre amour
N'est-il là niché!   18

Estaminet du Jeune Renard, août 1872

Chevaux de Bois

Par Saint-Gille,
Viens-nous-en,
Mon agile
Alezan.
  V. Hugo

Tournez, tournez, bons chevaux de bois,
Tournez cent tours, tournez mille tours,
Tournez souvent et tournez toujours,
Tournez, tournez au son des hautbois.   4

Le gros soldat, la plus grosse bonne
Sont sur vos dos comme dans leur chambre;
Car, en ce jour, au bois de la Cambre,
Les maîtres sont tous deux en personne.   8

Tournez, tournez, chevaux de leur cœur,
Tandis qu'autour de tous vos tournois
Clignote l'œil du filou sournois,
Tournez au son du piston vainqueur.   12

C'est ravissant comme ça vous soûle,
D'aller ainsi dans ce cirque bête!
Bien dans le ventre et mal dans la tête,
Du mal en masse et du bien en foule.   16

Tournez, tournez, sans qu'il soit besoin
D'user jamais de nuls éperons
Pour commander à vos galops ronds,
Tournez, tournez, sans espoir de foin.   20

Et dépêchez, chevaux de leur âme :
Déjà, voici que la nuit qui tombe
Va réunir pigeon et colombe,
Loin de la foire et loin de madame.   24

Tournez, tournez ! le ciel en velours
D'astres en or se vêt lentement.
Voici partir l'amante et l'amant.
Tournez au son joyeux des tambours.   28

Champ de foire de Saint-Gilles, août 1872

MALINES

Vers les prés le vent cherche noise
Aux girouettes, détail fin
Du château de quelque échevin,
Rouge de brique et bleu d'ardoise,
Vers les prés clairs, les prés sans fin . . .   5

Comme les arbres des féeries,
Des frênes, vagues frondaisons,
Echelonnent mille horizons
A ce Sahara de prairies,
Trèfle, luzerne et blancs gazons.   10

Les wagons filent en silence
Parmi ces sites apaisés.
Dormez, les vaches ! Reposez,
Doux taureaux de la plaine immense,
Sous vos cieux à peine irisés !   15

Le train glisse sans un murmure,
Chaque wagon est un salon
Où l'on cause bas et d'où l'on
Aime à loisir cette nature
Faite à souhait pour Fénelon.   20

Août 1872

Birds in the Night

Vous n'avez pas eu toute patience,
Cela se comprend par malheur, de reste ;
Vous êtes si jeune ! et l'insouciance,
C'est le lot amer de l'âge céleste !   4

Vous n'avez pas eu toute la douceur,
Cela par malheur d'ailleurs se comprend ;
Vous êtes si jeune, ô ma froide sœur,
Que votre cœur doit être indifférent !   8

Aussi me voici plein de pardons chastes,
Non, certes ! joyeux, mais très calme, en somme,
Bien que je déplore, en ces mois néfastes,
D'être, grâce à vous, le moins heureux homme.   12

                    *   *   *

Et vous voyez bien que j'avais raison,
Quand je vous disais, dans mes moments noirs,
Que vos yeux, foyer de mes vieux espoirs,
Ne couvaient plus rien que la trahison.   16

Vous juriez alors que c'était mensonge
Et votre regard qui mentait lui-même
Flambait comme un feu mourant qu'on prolonge,
Et de votre voix vous disiez : "Je t'aime !"   20

Hélas ! on se prend toujours au désir
Qu'on a d'être heureux malgré la saison . . .

Mais ce fut un jour plein d'amer plaisir,
Quand je m'aperçus que j'avais raison! 24

* * *

Aussi bien pourquoi me mettrais-je à geindre?
Vous ne m'aimiez pas, l'affaire est conclue,
Et, ne voulant pas qu'on ose me plaindre,
Je souffrirai d'une âme résolue. 28

Oui, je souffrirai car je vous aimais!
Mais je souffrirai comme un bon soldat
Blessé, qui s'en va dormir à jamais,
Plein d'amour pour quelque pays ingrat. 32

Vous qui fûtes ma Belle, ma Chérie,
Encor que de vous vienne ma souffrance,
N'êtes-vous donc pas toujours ma Patrie,
Aussi jeune, aussi folle que la France? 36

* * *

Or, je ne veux pas, —le puis-je d'abord?
Plonger dans ceci mes regards mouillés.
Pourtant mon amour que vous croyez mort
A peut-être enfin les yeux dessillés. 40

Mon amour qui n'est que ressouvenance,
Quoique sous vos coups il saigne et qu'il pleure
Encore et qu'il doive, à ce que je pense,
Souffrir longtemps jusqu'à ce qu'il en meure, 44

Peut-être a raison de croire entrevoir
En vous un remords qui n'est pas banal,
Et d'entendre dire, en son désespoir,
A votre mémoire: ah! fi! que c'est mal! 48

* * *

Je vous vois encor. J'entr'ouvris la porte.
Vous étiez au lit comme fatiguée.
Mais, ô corps léger que l'amour emporte,
Vous bondîtes nue, éplorée et gaie. 52

O quels baisers, quels enlacements fous!
J'en riais moi-même à travers mes pleurs.
Certes, ces instants seront entre tous,
Mes plus tristes, mais aussi mes meilleurs.   56

Je ne veux revoir de votre sourire
Et de vos bons yeux en cette occurrence
Et de vous, enfin, qu'il faudrait maudire,
Et du piège exquis, rien que l'apparence.   60

*   *   *

Je vous vois encore! En robe d'été
Blanche et jaune avec des fleurs de rideaux.
Mais vous n'aviez plus l'humide gaîté
Du plus délirant de tous nos tantôts.   64

La petite épouse et la fille aînée
Etait reparue avec la toilette
Et c'était déjà notre destinée
Qui me regardait sous votre voilette.   68

Soyez pardonnée! Et c'est pour cela
Que je garde, hélas! avec quelque orgueil,
En mon souvenir qui vous cajola,
L'éclair de côté que coulait votre œil.   72

*   *   *

Par instants je suis le pauvre navire
Qui court démâté parmi la tempête,
Et ne voyant pas Notre-Dame luire
Pour l'engouffrement en priant s'apprête.   76

Par instants je meurs la mort du pécheur
Qui se sait damné s'il n'est confessé,
Et, perdant l'espoir de nul confesseur,
Se tord dans l'Enfer qu'il a devancé.   80

O mais! par instants, j'ai l'extase rouge
Du premier chrétien, sous la dent rapace,

Qui rit à Jésus témoin, sans que bouge
Un poil de sa chair, un nerf de sa face! 84

Bruxelles–Londres—Septembre–octobre 1872

Aquarelles

GREEN

Voici des fruits, des fleurs, des feuilles et des branches,
Et puis voici mon cœur, qui ne bat que pour vous.
Ne le déchirez pas avec vos deux mains blanches
Et qu'à vos yeux si beaux l'humble présent soit doux. 4

J'arrive tout couvert encore de rosée
Que le vent du matin vient glacer à mon front.
Souffrez que ma fatigue, à vos pieds reposée,
Rêve des chers instants qui la délasseront. 8

Sur votre jeune sein laissez rouler ma tête
Toute sonore encor de vos derniers baisers;
Laissez-la s'apaiser de la bonne tempête,
Et que je dorme un peu puisque vous reposez. 12

SPLEEN

Les roses étaient toutes rouges,
Et les lierres étaient tout noirs.

Chère, pour peu que tu te bouges,
Renaissent tous mes désespoirs. 4

Le ciel était trop bleu, trop tendre,
La mer trop verte et l'air trop doux.

Je crains toujours, —ce qu'est d'attendre!—
Quelque fuite atroce de vous.   8

Du houx à la feuille vernie
Et du luisant buis je suis las,

Et de la campagne infinie
Et de tout, fors de vous, hélas!   12

STREETS

i

Dansons la gigue!

J'aimais surtout ses jolis yeux,
Plus clairs que l'étoile des cieux,
J'aimais ses yeux malicieux.   4

Dansons la gigue!

Elle avait des façons vraiment
De désoler un pauvre amant,
Que c'en était vraiment charmant!   8

Dansons la gigue!

Mais je trouve encore meilleur
Le baiser de sa bouche en fleur,
Depuis qu'elle est morte à mon cœur.   12

Dansons la gigue!

Je me souviens, je me souviens
Des heures et des entretiens,
Et c'est le meilleur de mes biens.   16

Dansons la gigue!

SOHO

ii

O la rivière dans la rue!
Fantastiquement apparue
Derrière un mur haut de cinq pieds,   3
Elle roule sans un murmure
Son onde opaque et pourtant pure,
Par les faubourgs pacifiés.   6

La chaussée est très large, en sorte
Que l'eau jaune comme une morte
Dévale ample et sans nuls espoirs   9
De rien refléter que la brume,
Même alors que l'aurore allume
Les cottages jaunes et noirs.   12

PADDINGTON

CHILD WIFE

Vous n'avez rien compris à ma simplicité,
   Rien, ô ma pauvre enfant!
Et c'est avec un front éventé, dépité,
   Que vous fuyez devant.   4

Vos yeux qui ne devaient refléter que douceur,
   Pauvre cher bleu miroir,
Ont pris un ton de fiel, ô lamentable sœur,
   Qui nous fait mal à voir.   8

Et vous gesticulez avec vos petits bras
   Comme un héros méchant,
En poussant d'aigres cris poitrinaires, hélas!
   Vous qui n'étiez que chant!   12

Car vous avez eu peur de l'orage et du cœur
   Qui grondait et sifflait,
Et vous bêlâtes vers votre mère—ô douleur!—
   Comme un triste agnelet.   16

Et vous n'avez pas su la lumière et l'honneur
   D'un amour brave et fort,
Joyeux dans le malheur, grave dans le bonheur,
   Jeune jusqu'à la mort!   20

A POOR YOUNG SHEPHERD

J'ai peur d'un baiser
Comme d'une abeille.
Je souffre et je veille
Sans me reposer.
J'ai peur d'un baiser!   5

Pourtant j'aime Kate
Et ses yeux jolis.
Elle est délicate
Aux longs traits pâlis.
Oh! que j'aime Kate!   10

C'est Saint-Valentin!
Je dois et je n'ose
Lui dire au matin . . .
La terrible chose
Que Saint-Valentin!   15

Elle m'est promise,
Fort heureusement!
Mais quelle entreprise
Que d'être un amant
Près d'une promise!   20

J'ai peur d'un baiser
Comme d'une abeille.
Je souffre et je veille
Sans me reposer.
J'ai peur d'un baiser!   25

BEAMS

Elle voulut aller sur les flots de la mer,
Et comme un vent bénin soufflait une embellie,
Nous nous prêtâmes tous à sa belle folie,
Et nous voilà marchant par le chemin amer.   4

Le soleil luisait haut dans le ciel calme et lisse,
Et dans ses cheveux blonds c'étaient des rayons d'or,
Si bien que nous suivions son pas plus calme encor
Que le déroulement des vagues, ô délice!   8

Des oiseaux blancs volaient alentour mollement,
Et des voiles au loin s'inclinaient toutes blanches.
Parfois de grands varechs filaient en longues branches,
Nos pieds glissaient d'un pur et large mouvement.   12

Elle se retourna, doucement inquiète
De ne nous croire pas pleinement rassurés;
Mais nous voyant joyeux d'être ses préférés,
Elle reprit sa route et portait haut la tête.   16

Douvres-Ostende, à bord de la *Comtesse-de-Flandre*,
4 avril 1873

COMMENTARIES

The text chosen is the *second edition*. The first edition has such a large number of printing errors that it would have to be edited in order to make it acceptable. The second edition (1887) is somewhat better than the third (1891), but even so contains a small number of mistakes. These have been rectified in accordance with the editions established by Borel and Robichez.

ARIETTES OUBLIEES

i. *C'est l'extase langoureuse . . .*

This poem was first published in the *Renaissance littéraire et artistique* on 18 May 1872 under the title 'Romance sans paroles'. Robichez, p. 580, gives the title in the singular: *romance . . .* ; Borel, in both the Pléiade edition, p. 1100, and the Gallimard 'Poésie' edition, p. 180, gives it in the plural. The difference appears minimal but is not without a certain relevance to the possible dates of composition of the 'Ariettes' as a whole, since the choice of the plural form would be an indication that other poems from the section are already contemplated if not completed; it would therefore tend to corroborate the idea that the sequence of 'Ariettes' was indeed written in the May-June period as Verlaine seems to indicate. The question is discussed at some length in Robichez, pp. 133–5 and Borel 'Poésie' pp. 175–6.

The epigraph is taken from Favart's *Ninette à la cour ou le Caprice amoureux* (given in March 1756) of which Verlaine possessed a copy. His interest in Favart was apparently stimulated by Rimbaud as Verlaine's letter of 2 April 1872 confirms: 'C'est charmant, l'*Ariette oubliée*, paroles et musique! Je me le suis fait déchiffrer et chanter! Merci de ce délicat envoi!' The significance of the epigraph does not lie in its original context, though it could be argued that four at least of the lines of Ninette's aria are relevant to one of the central preoccupations of the 'Ariettes oubliées', namely:

> Mais comme un Feuillage
> Qu'un vent ravage,
> Vos Cœurs sont agités,
> Vos Cœurs sont tourmentés,

but in the context Verlaine chooses to give it. It cannot be dismissed simply as 'dépourvue de toute signification précise' (Robichez, p. 580).

Its presence can be explained satisfactorily in terms of its literal meaning: Verlaine uses the epigraph to introduce the poem at that instant which follows the dying away of the wind, an instant alive with the small yet numerous sounds of nature which, in their turn, serve to produce a sort of brief but intense prolongation of the wind's effect. It is possible, of course, that Verlaine intended the epigraph to have a more esoteric meaning, but it is futile to look for one since the obvious meaning of the poem (by which is meant its fairly literal meaning) is well enough served by the epigraph as it stands.

Opening with a series of affirmations the poem creates a mood of a definite kind, akin to a feeling of physical/emotional satisfaction. The reiteration of 'c'est' is deliberately forceful. Yet the feeling the poem expresses, for all its deliberateness, is curiously fragile; its ingredients are an unorthodox mixture of vague sensation—'l'extase langoureuse'—of more explicit bodily pleasure—'la fatigue amoureuse'—and of various external objects (to use the word loosely)—'frissons des bois', 'brises', 'ramures grises' and 'petites voix'. These objects are precise enough to provide an elementary, and elemental, setting of a primary auditory/visual sort. At the same time, they are not unadorned statements of 'fact'. In the context of the opening two lines neither 'frissons' nor 'étreinte' could be considered objective. While one of their functions is the establishment of a recognisable natural framework—however sketchy it may be—their other and equally important function is the way in which they sustain the sensuous/sensual meaning of 'la fatigue amoureuse'. As well as reinforcing the general mood they also provide the means whereby it is gradually refined in the sense that, whereas the mood is somewhat diffused and imprecise when it is introduced in the first two lines, the bringing in of specific 'objects' acts immediately as a corrective to what might have become an excessive vagueness and abstraction. The objects are not produced at random. As the poem progresses there is a gradual narrowing of focus. So that while it is doubtless true to say that the feeling of 'extase' is meant to draw every detail into its orbit (in the opening stanza, that is), it is equally evident that the channelling of the feeling of 'extase' into and through the various objects is a necessary step towards the eventual resolution, if such it is, of the poem's mood.

The second verse continues both the affirmative nature of the first and the gradual 'descent' to more specific details: 'frissons des bois' has moved through 'ramures grises' to the 'herbe agitée' and the 'cailloux'. In addition, the sounds which the words suggest have also moved from the general to the particular, the 'frissons' have become 'petites voix' and have finally resolved into a 'cri doux' and the 'roulis sourd'. Here again, the

cri doux
Que l'herbe agitée expire

maintains the amorous connotations of verse 1. But this stanza does more than provide a continuation of the early mood; it acts as a pivot. The mood's certainty begins to break up, at first almost imperceptibly as Verlaine introduces a term of comparison—'cela *ressemble* . . .'— which moves the poem fractionally away from saying 'this is' to saying 'this is like . . .'. The movement becomes more rapid as the indicative gives way to a conditional 'tu dirais'. What has happened is that the poet has begun the process of withdrawal from his total involvement in the initial mood to a position in which he starts to reflect upon the mood. As this continues, the poem's focus clears. From a general diffusion of sentiment, of which the poet was a seemingly integral part, the poem succeeds in introducing a distinction between the poet's changing feelings and the projection of those feelings on to the immediate surroundings. As the differentiation becomes more sharp, so the mood becomes less certain, less affirmative. At the end of the stanza the poem's change of direction is confirmed by the introduction of a person assumed to have been sharing the poet's mood.

The final verse carries the uncertainty to its conclusion and the poem finishes on a note of unease. The assurance of verse 1 has disappeared. The sounds of nature, themselves unchanged, assume a different meaning directly related to the poet's changing frame of mind. The pleasure vanishes (though not entirely?) and is replaced by 'cette âme qui se lamente'. The last three lines of the poem represent an unhappy attempt to find again the opening unity; they try to draw together the 'humble antienne', the poet and the poet's silent companion. The attempt is a failure simply because in this particular poem the mere fact of actually distinguishing the three 'ingredients' means that the unity is broken. From harmony the poem falls into dissonance; from peace of mind to disquiet. Conscious reflection—in this case arising from feelings of anxiety about the companion and about the nature of the relationship, its closeness, the reciprocation of feelings—dispels, or at least disrupts the trance-like state in which the poem starts.

If a meaning has to be found for the poem then it derives from the way in which the poem, admittedly on a miniature scale, copies the patterns of normal existence: the insidious invasion of personal happiness by vague feelings of doubt culminating in implied disillusion. Verlaine's expression of it is unique (and it is not necessarily a deliberate choice); but it is indeed this common pattern of experience which contributes in a large, and unacknowledged, degree to the special potency of this *ariette*.

ii. *Je devine, a travers un murmure . . .*

The first known version of the poem dates from a letter to Emile
Blémont of 22 September 1872. Verlaine gives it a title: 'Escarpolette'.
Originally there was an epigraph, a quotation from the *Iliad*, which was
struck out on the manuscript and did not appear in any of the printed
editions (see Robichez, p. 581 and Borel, 'Pléiade', p. 1101). It consisted
of a fragment meaning 'let us now yield to black night'. Robichez
suggests, among other things, that Verlaine may have been referring to
the 'anéantissement de l'inconscience' (does he not mean 'conscience'?);
the proposition is attractive but seems to overlook the lucidity with
which Verlaine constructs the poem and also the bald fact that the
epigraph was eventually considered unnecessary.

The single concrete image in the poem is the swing. It occurs as the
last word yet it is the very word on which the entire poem is con-
structed. To begin with, the poem can be interpreted literally in terms
of a swinging motion: the first stanza shows the poet aware of sights and
sounds, of past and present and of the 'swing' between them; the middle
stanza represents his acute awareness of the movement itself to the point
where awareness of other things is completely blurred; the final stanza is
the return to a steadier movement and at the same time the expression
of the unfulfilled desire to perpetuate the state of mind of the middle
verse. That the poem could indeed be said to follow a 'swinging' curve
is further emphasised by something as commonplace as punctuation.
Verlaine's use of it turns out to be consistent with the idea of an increase
in movement in the middle verse followed by a gradual slowing down.
The first and third verses are end-stopped in three out of four lines—in
the first to allow for a series of 'factual' statements and in the third to
give time for reminiscence. The second verse is without punctuation
except for the last line. Such an arrangement would appear to corre-
spond (not that the correspondence is rigid) with the sense of increasing
movement and its accompanying sense of decreasing reflective
consciousness.

The opening verse refers to 'voix anciennes' and then to an 'aurore
future'. In spite of an evident desire to draw them together the poet
realises that each has its separate existence. In the third verse there is
equally the recognition that 'jeunes et vieilles heures' never were, and
never can be, identical. Such a distinction simply does not exist in the
second verse. There, the different elements are fused—not to say
confused.

Nothing in this poem is explicit. Verlaine offers no ready explanation.
The reader has no alternative but to accept at face value a straightfor-
ward statement, grammatically, that is. The syntactical simplicity serves

as a vehicle for a vagueness that refuses to be penetrated. Sounds heard and sounds remembered seem to come from the same source, the one shading into the other. The use of the word 'contour'—highly unusual—for all its clarity, scarcely serves to dispel the already blurred outline. In fact, Verlaine's next step is to prevent even the very precarious image that 'contour' offered from ever crystallising; 'subtil' and then 'anciennes' effectively operate against any momentary impression of precision. The remaining two lines are no clearer. They can be *understood*; Verlaine indulges in no syntactical camouflage, but he keeps his real meaning well hidden, always assuming that there is a meaning somewhere behind the surface. The stanza is nicely patterned; individual words can be seen to balance others in the verse; sounds echo one another; the whole structure is a tightly-woven tapestry of interrelated meanings. There is, without question, an *impression* of clarity. Yet, as was the case in the first *ariette*, there is no precise meaning; and no precise meaning exists in spite of the number of interpretations which have been advanced. What the stanza is 'about' is the growing feeling of what might roughly be described as optimism, a growth traceable through the 'voix anciennes' to the 'aurore future'. The 'meaning' of the stanza is in this very movement; is in the increasing intensity of the feelings expressed.

The middle stanza prolongs the sentiment of (pleasurable) intensity. For a brief moment all distinction between past and present is abolished. Everything is confused in a state of vertigo. But the moment quickly fades with the poet's rather ironic reflection on his delirium, 'l'ariette, hélas! de toutes lyres!', a comment which exposes the feeling for the day-dreaming it was. There is, however, a problem relating to the meaning of the last line of this stanza. Does 'de toutes lyres' imply that the poet's indecision, resulting from the pull of opposites, leaves him open to every influence? Or does it speak, as some would have it, of impersonality—'le moi se fond au chant universel; il se sent impersonnel' (Nadal, p. 51); 'la voix d'un lyrisme impersonnel' (Richard, p. 176)—and the added implication that the poet is abdicating his own individuality?

The final stanza provides a logical conclusion. 'Hélas!' was the point at which the poet began to distance himself from his own mood. Once outside his mood it vanishes rapidly. But the disappearance of the mood is not accompanied by any heroics. To say that the diminutives 'cachent l'acuité de l'angoisse' (Zimmermann, p. 73) is to go too far. The poem is not an exercise in the grand manner. There is no death wish, no literal passing away. There is, however, a wry literary gesture of resignation which is virtually self-explanatory: the poet wishes that the mood of the middle stanza would continue, but he cannot sustain it. The poem ends on the word which is its mainspring and its summing-up: the poet is still 'swinging', nothing has been resolved in the heady excitement of verse 2, nothing has been achieved.

Verlaine delicately traces a moment's upsurge of hopeful anticipation followed by its inevitable destruction and the accompanying sense of disappointment.

iii. *Il pleure dans mon cœur . . .*

The manuscript has two epigraphs, one from Longfellow's poem 'The Rainy Day', 'It rains, and the wind is never weary' (Robichez, p. 582, thinks that it is a late addition to the poem), and one, apparently, from Rimbaud, though its precise source, if it exists, has not been traced. Only the second survives in the published editions. In any case, the first is not entirely appropriate; the wind has no place in the poem, though similarities do exist as far as the general mood is concerned. For example, Longfellow has the following lines: 'My life is cold, and dark, and dreary . . . Be still, sad heart! and cease repining'; Longfellow's poem too depends on a great deal of repetition, though it is by no means as subtle as Verlaine's. Where the poems differ completely is in their intentions; Longfellow moralises in a way which, in the 'Ariettes' at least, is unthinkable for Verlaine. The last verse of Longfellow's poem bears quoting for its lack of poetic tact:

> Be still, sad heart! and cease repining;
> Behind the clouds is the sun still shining;
> Thy fate is the common fate of all,
> Into each life some rain must fall,
> Some days must be dark and dreary.

The exact date of composition of the *ariette* is unknown. Adam, without any substantial evidence, suggests October 1872.

The poem is as much concerned with conscious reflection as it is with expressing a state of mind. In its own way it conforms to the by now increasingly familiar pattern of affirmation followed by a more detached assessment. The pattern occurs in its entirety in the first verse and is repeated in verse two. The third and final verses are given over to comment. Unlike the previous *ariette* this one does not trace a curve of feeling; its domain is static and colourless, a sort of limbo of unchanging statement, question and lack of response—the cloud of grey drabness is never dispelled. All the mechanical devices, in so far as it serves a useful purpose to separate them out for special mention, underscore the sameness of feeling; Verlaine chooses deliberately monotonous repetitive effects—'cœur' is used five times and is picked up in 's'écœure'; the sound occurs again in 'pleure' and 'langueur' and can be linked with 'pleut'; the rhyme scheme is intentionally poverty-stricken, the second line of each stanza remaining without an echo—except that 'toits' finds a faint response in 'pourquoi'—and the last line of each stanza using the same rhyme word as the first. Even the scattering of exclamation marks and question marks does not seem to denote a heightening of tension or an intensification of mood. The former are indicative of sighs (without overdoing the effect; the poem is not an exercise in declamation), the latter of a weary, purposeless shrug—it seems essential, in order to preserve the overall tone of the poem, that all its ingredients should be as muted as possible.

The language itself is prosaic. The minimal concession to 'poetic' diction occurs in the opening line 'Il pleure dans mon cœur'—a sure introduction to the poetic world of melancholy and boredom—and Verlaine never goes beyond that. He catches a feeling of emptiness, of lack of movement, of lack of ideas, of lack of meaning. The feeling arrives unannounced, unwanted yet overpowering. It has no explanation. The poet's questions are feeble gestures without the strength to provide a way out of the mood. Instead, they only serve to prolong it. Confronted with his own dreary personality in a decor which offers no distractions, the poet sinks into a mindless and pointless sadness.

iv. *Il faut, voyez-vous, nous pardonner les choses . . .*

The epigraph is again dispensed with in the second edition. Originally Verlaine had taken a line from 'Lassitude' (*Poèmes Saturniens*): 'De la douceur, de la douceur, de la douceur' and had modestly or humorously (or cynically) added '(INCONNU)'. If it is intended that the earlier poem be consulted, what conclusions regarding this fourth *ariette* should be drawn from the expression of a desire for a calm, if deceiving, relationship with a woman who is essentially of a passionate and demonstrative nature which 'Lassitude' offers? The desire for a calm relationship is common to both poems, but the sensuality of the first poem is more than discreetly veiled in the *ariette*. Not only that, the relationship is presented here as if it were between two (young) women; or, if it is felt that it is going too far to see both participants as female, it is suggested that the quality of the feelings expressed, wished for even, should be essentially feminine.

It is evident that this *ariette* is of a different nature from that of the previous three. While exhibiting a similar disregard for visual details, it is still much more clear, more overtly anecdotal. Even so, Verlaine gets by, in no derogatory sense, on surprisingly little: there is virtually no colour—'pâlir' is as near as he comes to producing any; there is no sound, no touch, no smell. The poem operates in a sensual vacuum; it is a piece of wishful thinking. It is not without certain ambiguities.

The opening line raises questions that are never answered, questions concerning identity: to whom is the request directed; who are 'nous'; what needs forgiving? The forgiveness is not a fact of the poem, it is merely a hope. Having expressed the hope and having said how good it would be to be forgiven (a nod in the direction of conventional morality—the poem is usually interpreted as relating to Verlaine's relationship with Rimbaud) the poet turns to what is, after all, his principal preoccupation—his relationship with the chosen companion. Throughout the poem there is an emphasis on sharing; 'nous' occurs as an actual word six times and is consistently strengthened by related expressions, 'notre vie', 'nos vœux confus', 'deux pleureuses', 'âmes sœurs', 'deux enfants' and 'deux jeunes filles'. As the poem progresses there is a gradual withdrawal into the proposed shared world; other people are first relegated to the background (verse two), then forgotten altogether (verse three). Even the forgiveness originally asked for, and miraculously assumed to have been granted (?), becomes unimportant. It is replaced by an ever increasing emphasis on the couple's youthful innocence. It is precisely on this point that the poem achieves its greatest ambiguity because the innocence is presented in a context of implied wrong-doing. Why, otherwise, use 'pardonner'? The innocence is suspiciously like that of the *ingénue* whose perversity is masked under the cloak of harmless friendship; 'pâlir sous les chastes charmilles' is nothing if not an anticipation of pleasure.

The poem has its parentage in two—and possibly three—of Verlaine's earlier collections. The *Poèmes Saturniens* contains 'La Chanson des Ingénues'—a picture of knowing innocence anticipating, with some delight, its own eventual and inevitable seduction. The young girl in 'Initium' has an 'âme d'enfant', yet her eyes are full of a 'sensuelle ampleur'—the same mixture. Much more explicitly, the series of sonnets in *Parallèlement*, 'Les Amies' (completed at the latest by the autumn of 1867) combines extreme innocence with extreme sexuality. A feature of these erotic poems is the child-like quality of one of the participants and the associations with whiteness, paleness and candour. One of the images in the poem entitled 'Printemps' is the 'charmille', in this case not at all chaste:

> Ton enfance est une charmille:
> Laisse errer mes doigts dans la mousse
> Où le bouton de rose brille . . .

This *ariette* does not go anything like that far—but it implies a continuation on those lines. Of course, it *could* be innocent.

v. *Le piano que baise une main frêle . . .*

The poem was first published in the *Renaissance littéraire et artistique* of 29

June 1872 where it was entitled 'Ariette'. The epigraph is taken from Pétrus Borel's poem 'Doléance' (in *Rhapsodies*, Levavasseur, 1832, pp. 73–5; the most readily available edition of the *Rhapsodies* is in the Slatkine Reprint, Geneva, 1967, in the *Œuvres complètes*, vol. ii) which begins:

> Son joyeux, importun, d'un clavecin sonore,
>> Parle, que me veux-tu?
> Viens-tu, dans mon grenier, pour insulter encore
>> A ce cœur abattu?
> Son joyeux, ne viens plus; verse à d'autres l'ivresse;
>> Leur vie est un festin
> Que je n'ai point troublé; tu troubles ma détresse,
>> Mon râle clandestin!
>
> Indiscret, d'où viens-tu? Sans doute une main blanche,
>> Un beau doigt prisonnier
> Dans de riches joyaux a frappé sur ton anche
>> D'ivoire et d'ébénier . . .

Pétrus Borel was evidently one of Verlaine's preferred authors. For an assessment of his possible influence see G. Zayed, *La Formation littéraire de Verlaine*, pp. 292–7. These opening lines contain in essence the main ideas in Verlaine's *ariette*.

With this *ariette* the poet returns to the tried technique of statement followed by a question (or questions). The setting, though minimal, is explicit enough: a piano, being quietly played, in a 'boudoir' with its window 'ouverte un peu sur le petit jardin'. There, however, the definition ends, because the poet is concerned with blurring any outline that might tend to become too precise. This he does by choosing as his central image 'un air bien vieux, bien faible et bien charmant'. The melody is 'doux', 'discret', 'fin', 'incertain'; it barely exists in fact; and in the poem is in any case on the point of fading away altogether. For the reader, of course, it remains unheard and, to borrow an idea, all the sweeter for not materialising. Even the pianist is scarcely real. And the woman's pervading presence is reduced to a scent, even though it is obviously the most important feature of the poem in as much as the poet's attempt to rationalise the impact of the music on his feelings is an indirect attempt to work out his relationship with the woman.

The first stanza is presented in an 'objective' manner; the poet makes a series of statements uncoloured by (overt) personal reflections. It is none the less apparent that the poet is very much at the centre of things simply because the 'descriptions' verge on the fringe of unreality and partake as much of a dreamlike world as they do of an ordinary domestic setting. The latter is recognisably there, but its importance—

apart from providing another of Verlaine's flimsy frameworks—lies in its transformation into a totally subjective mood picture. It is as though the poet were in a soporific state of mind, barely conscious of anything other than those sights, sounds, smells which encourage him to remain in a state of pleasurable drowsiness. He acquiesces in the passive reciprocation of his own mood with that of his immediate surroundings; his critical sense is lulled into a phase of inactivity. Such, roughly speaking, is the general effect of the stanza, achieved, let it be said, by a totally lucid and controlled choice of every word; nothing is out of place, everything contributes to the creation of the overall mood. It is a question of deliberate artistry producing the vaguest of 'pictures'.

The second stanza provides a shift in focus and mood as the poet tries, unsuccessfully—or at least inconclusively—to understand the meaning, if any, of what he was experiencing. Having stepped outside his mood— far enough to question it but not far enough to see it in any rational perspective—he succeeds in fragmenting his experience without being able to produce a new pattern to replace the old one. Probing the vagueness of his original mood only serves to make it more difficult to interpret. The poet finds that the vagueness of the mood is matched by the uncertainty of his response to it. Here again, however, Verlaine's skill as a technician never deserts him: the tense sequence accurately captures the poet's changing and unsure reaction. The present tense: 'qu'est-ce que c'est . . .' is his first reflection. With it goes the recognition that he was, in some obscure and evidently unacceptable way being 'possessed' by the music, like a child being rocked to sleep in a cradle. The conditional: 'que voudrais-tu?' expresses a certain perplexed surprise—as if the poet were trying to deny that he had ever been under the music's spell. The moment passes; 'qu'as-tu voulu?' comes almost too late; the music has exercised its momentary charm and passed on.

It is scarcely true to say, as Borel does ('Pléiade', pp. 178-9), that there is a 'destruction quasi totale de l'architecture du poème et de son armature logique'. That is to mistake the effect for the cause. Verlaine's preference for the most ephemeral states of mind, and his convincing expression of them, is the result of a highly developed poetic instinct coupled with an almost infallible ability to choose the right words. No *art* is more logical, though no moods are more vague.

vi. *C'est le chien de Jean de Nivelle . . .*

Of all the *ariettes* this one is the most problematical. In its immediate context it appears out of place. Robichez (p. 586) puts forward a neat solution (assuming that it is essential to insist on the underlying unity of the 'Ariettes'): 'on a vu dans les trois premières [ariettes] s'abolir intentions, sentiments clairs et concepts dans une sorte de vide intérieur où ne subsistait qu'une vague tonalité générale. La situation de l'écrivain public, qui n'écrit jamais une ligne qui le concerne, n'est que le cas-limite où ce vide se trouve intégralement réalisé'. Zimmermann, on the other hand, tends to see in the poem a 'divertissement', put in to 'changer le ton, chasser la mélancolie' (p. 59). Whatever its real meaning, it is the only poem which deliberately uses sources outside itself—mainly folklore and popular song. Simply, therefore, for information, the following notes may provide some assistance in the poem's interpretation.

l. 1. Jean de Nivelle (1422–77?) was the eldest son of Jean II de Montmorency. According to popular legend he refused to obey his father and march against the Duke of Burgundy—from which 'fact' emerged the saying, 'il ressemble au (= à ce) chien de Jean de Nivelle qui s'enfuit quand on l'appelle'.

l. 3. La Mère Michel is a figure in folksong who loses her cat.

l. 14. Lustucru, described as a 'type populaire de personnage niais' turns up in a song as a baker.

l. 7. Angélique, the heroine (or one of them) of Ariosto's *Orlando furioso*, is struck by Cupid's arrow and, as a result, prefers Médor to all her other suitors and marries him (Zayed, p. 124, says that Verlaine was more likely to have come across the pair of lovers in the work of the French composer of comic operas Ambroise Thomas than in the original version. Thomas did in fact write a one-act comic opera called *Angélique et Médor* in 1843. It was never very popular. Verlaine may have seen an old poster rather than the work itself).

The remaining two characters (Monsieur Loss apart (l. 24); this is a distorted version of the name of the financier John Law) are less simple. La Ramée (l. 9) is possibly a reference to a character of the same name in Molière's *Don Juan*. There he is called a *bretteur* or *spadassin*, a swordsman, someone who enjoys fighting, a bully—but his actual role in the play is virtually non-existent. Robichez (p. 585) says La Ramée is a 'surnom de troupier galant'—which is appropriate enough for this poem. Why he should wear an 'habit blanc' which is 'mal famé' is not clear. François-les-bas-bleus (l. 4), the hero of the poem, is presumably taken from Charles Nodier's short story *Jean-François les bas-bleus*. By normal standards he is an idiot, though he is also a person of considerable perception and vision, a man whose madness is brought about by unrequited love and who dies, inexplicably, at the very moment the girl he loves is guillotined.

To add further to the jumble of references line 22: 'Car tant d'or s'y relève en bosse' has been lifted from Molière's *Les Femmes savantes*, Act III, scene ii (Trissotin's speech). But Molière himself appears to have lifted it from Cotin's *Œuvres galantes* (it was Cotin himself whom Molière was attacking in the character of Trissotin):

> L'amour si chèrement m'a vendu son lien
> Qu'il m'en coûte déjà la moitié de mon bien;
> Et, quand tu vois ce beau carrosse
> Où tant d'or se relève en bosse
> Qu'il étonne tout le pays
> Et fait pompeusement triompher ma Laïs,
> Ne dis plus qu'il est amarante,
> Dis plutôt qu'il est de ma rente.

There are other details connected with meaning. What does *verdir* mean in l. 8? Does it refer to a drawing, a statue, a poster, perhaps? Is one of these growing old and mouldy, as it were, on a wall? Robichez follows Zayed in assuming that Verlaine had discovered Médor and Angélique 'à travers quelque vieille chanson' (p. 585). That is certainly possible, but, as Zayed himself has pointed out (p. 47) Ariosto was one of the authors Verlaine appears to have had some knowledge of. In which case it seems reasonable to take the text of the *Orlando furioso* and see whether or not there is a likely source for the image Verlaine uses. There was no shortage of recent French translations of Ariosto. Two prose versions, one of 1839 by M. A. Mazuy and one of 1844 by V. Philipon de la Madeleine, were available as were two verse versions, the earliest from 1834 by the Baron de Frenilly and the other, by C. H. Duvan de Chavagne, was published in 1838. And in fact, in Canto xix, stanza 36 goes as follows:

> Fra piacer tanti, ovunque un arbor dritto
> vedesse ombrare o fonte o rivo puro,
> v'avea spillo o coltel subito fitto;
> così, se v'era alcun sasso men duro:
> et era fuori in mille luoghi scritto,
> e così in casa in altritanti il muro,
> Angelica e Medoro, in varii modi
> legati insieme di diversi nodi.

the English translation from Sir John Harington's version (still available) is:

> Amid these joyes (as great as joyes might be)
> Their manner was on ev'ry wall within,
> Without on ev'ry stone or shady tree,
> To grave their names with bodkin, knife or pin,
> *Angelica* and *Medore*, you plaine might see,
> (So great a glory had they both therein)
> *Angelica* and *Medore* in ev'ry place,
> With sundry knots and wreathes they interlace.

Verlaine's image of the two names going green with age is therefore not entirely unexpected.

Verse four surely indicates that the *boulangère* has just favoured La Ramée's passion ('couronné sa flamme') and *not* Bernant Lustucru's (if naïve, then probably a cuckold).

And who is the 'impure' of verse five?

Having assembled the characters as well as one can, what is to be made of them? They come and go without any apparent reason, only François-les-bas-bleus remains as the one permanent figure, a curiously detached onlooker, indifferent to the antics of the poem's motley crew, except that he finds them amusing. No really comprehensible pattern emerges. Outside the poem the various figures have no connection whatsoever with each other. Yet for all the fantasy of this pantomime-like world, there is a central 'subject'—a subject which underlies the other *ariettes* as well—that of love. Here, however, it is either forgotten or faded; it is adulterous or it sells itself to the highest bidder. François observes it in its various guises, finds it something to smile at, and stays basically unmoved (because of the purity of his own love?). If the figure of François is meant as a disguise for the poet, then he achieves a rare detachment of feeling arrived at, one suspects, because of the choice of unreal figures around him and because he himself is an idiot. He still represents just as transparently the poet's abdication of his critical faculties and his inability to make sense of his feelings. Again it is the question of personal relationships which is the most important aspect of the poem and again they are shown as unsatisfactory (and debased).

vii. *O triste, triste était mon âme . . .*

This *ariette* poses no problems. It returns to familiar ground and familiar techniques: the first four couplets provide a direct statement of the poet's feelings and the last four search for an explanation of the feelings. As usual no explanations are forthcoming. The dialogue between the 'cœur' and the 'âme' produces questions not answers. The reasons for the poet's sadness have, in a sense, to stay undiscovered.

The distress is described as something in the past which, inexplicably, is still influencing the poet's present mood. The basic situation is one of separation, but though this is the direct cause of the poet's unhappiness he seems unable to believe in the actual fact of separation. The emotional unrest communicates itself to the poet's rational self. The poet's mind, however conscious it is of the gap between what is real (separation) and what seems real (the continued presence of the woman), is powerless to work out an explanation while at the same time desperately needing to find one. The poet is caught in his customary dilemma: his emotions are too strong for him to overcome them, but not strong enough to prevent him from detaching himself from them in order to call them into question. What he fails to do is put them into a perspective that makes sense. As a result, the poem ends on a note of disquiet.

viii. *Dans l'interminable* . . .

The characteristics of this *ariette* are those which are generally considered typical of Verlaine's best poetry—the predilection for an impressionistic 'paysage', the use of 'vers impairs' and the frequent exploitation of repetitive devices. This poem, too, follows the pattern of statement/question, affirmation/uncertainty.

The impressionism is dependent on the introduction of just sufficient details to suggest a coherent picture, albeit vague. The details themselves are for the most part rather generalised, 'plaine', 'neige', 'sable', 'ciel', 'lune' . . . When Verlaine requires a clearer focus the details become more specific, 'chêne', 'corneille', 'loups' . . . but he never allows a well-defined picture to emerge. Words which might conceivably suggest clear outlines have their edges softened by being paired with words that convey no sense of shape—'interminable', 'incertaine', 'buées'. Nor are the verbs any help—'luit', 'croirait voir', 'mourir', 'flottent'. The result is a landscape of disturbing irreality where a ghostly, impalpable moon, disembodied trees and morbidly unhealthy creatures come and go seemingly at random. Yet the whole series of vague, uneasy images is caught in a relatively ordinary grammatical web, itself tightened by the closely patterned structure of the poem as a whole—A B C B D A. In terms of its comparative simplicity the poem's syntax turns out to be an admirable vehicle for the *effect* of vagueness. The precision of the technique is placed at the service of a feeling that is far from precise. Verlaine was obviously fond of the apparent contradiction in means and ends. But the vagueness always works at the level of the *impression* the poem makes. In the poem's actual presentation there is nothing if not fairly cold logic. Every element is carefully thought out; even the question near the end of the poem serves to reinforce at the syntactical level the doubt—the word is used loosely—which is already there at the representational and emotional level.

The poem creates a mood of bleakness, unrelieved except for small eddies of brief interest on the uniformly grey surface, a mood which establishes itself unremittingly in the final stanza, a mood both inescapable and inexplicable.

ix. *L'ombre des arbres dans la rivière embrumée* . . .

The epigraph is self-explanatory. Its source is in Cyrano de Bergerac's

Lettres satiriques et amoureuses from the *Œuvres comiques*. Verlaine may have known the two-volume publication of 1858, of the *Œuvres de Cyrano de Bergerac*, nouvelle éd. revue et publiée par P. L. Jacob, 'Bibliothèque gauloise', Delahays.

The poem, too, requires virtually no explanation. For the first time in these *ariettes* Verlaine is more concerned to provide a 'rational' poem than to establish a mood though he does, of course, create a mood in line with that of the other poems in this section. He writes in such a way as to draw attention to the deliberate paralleling of verse two with verse one. 'Tandis qu'en l'air, parmi les ramures réelles' is neatly balanced by 'dans les hautes feuillées'; 'se plaignent' is echoed by 'tristes pleuraient' and 'les tourterelles' becomes 'tes espérances' ('tourterelles' = 'espérances' relates the poem to the love theme running through most of the *ariettes*).

The poem acts as a pendant to the whole section, underlining as it does both the concern with structure and the expression of feelings by means of the 'paysage'. It may not have been Verlaine's intention to give such a concise summary of the *ariettes*, but this poem admirably fills that function, closing the sequence with a finality that is only too obviously missing from the previous poems.

PAYSAGES BELGES

The epigraph serves the two poems 'Walcourt' and 'Charleroi'. Its meaning is not clear unless one adopts Robichez's explanation based on Verlaine's wanderings with Rimbaud: 'les deux voyageurs sont animés de la même ardeur triomphante qu'un Louis XIV jeune partant à la conquête des Pays-Bas' (p. 588).

Walcourt

Dated July 1872 in the original edition, the poem was erroneously dated July 1873 in subsequent editions. One might begin by commenting on the poem's so-called impressionism. No doubt the poem conveys impressions of bustle and activity; no doubt too its impact is visual—though the point can be disputed—but any connection with painting technique proper is tenuous. It is probably more accurate to repeat what Borel has to say when he writes, 'la poésie de Verlaine n'est aucunement une transposition dans l'ordre du langage de l'art des peintres impressionnistes' ('Pléiade', p. 184). In any case, the poem contains no evidence of interest in colour as such. What colour there is comes indirectly through the nouns the poet uses; even then, exact colours are left to the reader's imagination.

The outstanding characteristics of this poem are the lack of verbs and the very deliberate patterning. It is the latter that is the most important feature of the poem. Each stanza, complete in itself, is built up on similar lines. Each contains a mixture of the same ingredients (in different quantities and in different positions) namely: a pair of nouns (the most variable feature), a place, an implicit comment on the nature and atmosphere of the place and a human interest. Yet for all the awareness of the carefully arranged structure of the poem, the structure has little value (technical prowess apart) except as a channel through which the feeling expressed can grow in intensity. As the scene changes, the intimacy of the 'petits asiles / Pour les amants' is enlarged and becomes, so to speak, more publicly embracing. The cosy niche for two changes to 'tentes' then to 'guinguettes' (pleasure gardens with music and dancing) and finally to 'gares' and the ever open road. The accompanying human figures, initially in twos, get gradually more numerous. The 'amants' are replaced by the 'francs buveurs'. In turn their place is taken by the 'servantes' and the 'fumeurs', while the final verse includes in its purview an even more wide-flung and heterogeneous group. As the numbers increase so does the noise and the activity.

The poem is the expression of a sort of explosion of joy. That is its 'meaning'. That is what distinguishes it from a mere display of technique. Without the impression of growth, without the sense of carefree expansion, the poem's worth on the level of composition (which must not, none the less, be underestimated) would be no more than that which can be derived from most clever but trivial word-spinning.

Almost as an afterthought it has to be pointed out that the poem contains its share of humour in the ambiguous use of 'insignes' (conspicuous/notorious), 'francs' (normally means frank/open; Littré comments that when it precedes the noun it qualifies it means 'vrai, véritable—mais avec une nuance ironique qui n'en fait pas un éloge'), and 'chères' (in both senses of dear?). The ambiguity only adds to the feeling of pleasure, providing a certain element of harmless amusement.

Charleroi

In its structure this 'paysage' is reminiscent of earlier poems. One of its more obvious functions is to serve as a companion piece to 'Walcourt'. Both poems exhibit Verlaine's expressed interest in 'modernism', though there is no explicit acknowledgement of this interest until the letter to Lepelletier from London of 24 September 1872—some two months after the recognised date for the completion of 'Walcourt' and 'Charleroi'—where Verlaine writes of the 'interminable docks (qui suffisent d'ailleurs à ma poétique de plus en plus *moderniste*) . . .'.

In 'Charleroi' the unpleasant nature of the industrial setting is compounded rather than offset by the reference to Kobolds which in old

German tales are set to guard subterranean treasures, the treasure in this case being coal. Their imagined presence adds to the sense of alienation and dehumanisation which Charleroi gives. Even those details which are reminders of human beings are repulsive:

> Plutôt des bouges
> Que des maisons;

> Oh! votre haleine,
> Sueur humaine.

The poet's reaction is one of bewilderment and confusion. Assaulted by noise ('l'avoine siffle . . . des gares tonnent . . . Quoi bruissait / Comme des sistres? . . . cris des métaux') and by unidentifiable smells ('Quoi donc se sent? . . . on sent donc quoi? . . . parfums sinistres') it is small wonder that 'les yeux s'étonnent'. The assault, in one instance, is literal:

> Un buisson gifle
> L'œil au passant.

In these circumstances the poet has little control over his reactions and no means whereby he can come to terms with them.

The poem's structure is less evidently well organised than that of 'Walcourt', but it is as equally expressive of the bewilderment and perplexity which the industrial landscape induces in the poet. Here, the stanzas offer no sense of progression. Instead they accumulate the noises, smells and sights in a relatively haphazard order as the poet's attention is drawn rapidly from one to another. Though the impressions are strong and vivid they are unwelcome. What is especially disconcerting is that even with familiar objects there is virtually no sense of familiarity; the grass is black, for example. The kaleidoscopic imagery shares something of the quality of a nightmare. And as the images recur (never exactly identical, though of a similar nature) the poet finds himself coming full circle and faced once more with the hallucinatory Kobolds. At this point the poem ends. The restatement of the opening verse is no doubt satisfactory from the point of view of composition, but from the emotional side the return to the opening image in no way compensates for the feeling of disorientation which has been produced. 'Charleroi' remains true to the procedure of the 'Ariettes oubliées'—questions without answers, feelings without reasons, 'ce côté effaré si propre à Verlaine' (Borel, 'Pléiade', p. 185).

Bruxelles: Simples Fresques i

A letter to Blémont, 22 September 1872, contains the first known state of the poem. Verlaine writes of 'une série que je nommerai: *De Charleroi à Londres*'. Apart from 'Simple Fresque' (which had an epigraph: 'Près de la ville de Bruxelles en Brabant. "Complainte d'Isaac Laquedem" ') the letter included 'Paysage Belge' (which became 'Simples Fresques ii' in the published version), 'Chevaux de Bois' and 'Escarpolette' ('Ariette oubliée' ii).

'Ces vers . . . peuvent compter parmi les plus mystérieux que Verlaine ait écrits' (Zimmermann, p. 301). Zimmermann is extremely fair in her remarks on the poem for, without wishing to detract from it, she makes it quite clear that there are a number of difficulties in the text which effectively prevent a reasonable interpretation: 'La *vision* créée est très moderne, dans un sens que Verlaine ne pouvait anticiper. On se croit devant une œuvre de Kokoschka, ou d'un peintre postérieur encore, lorsqu'on essaye de reconstruire mentalement ce tableau où des couleurs isolées ne qualifient aucun object concret . . . où les quelques esquisses de contours sont également désincarnées' (Zimmermann, p. 301). Without going into a detailed explanation Robichez (p. 590) puts forward the opinion that 'verdâtre' and 'rêvassent', both 'légèrement péjorative[s]', are responsible for the tone of the poem, a tone which, while obviously melancholic, contains an element of self-deflation. Maybe.

'Simples Fresques i' bears many of the marks of the characteristic Verlaine—'vers impair', a vague overall mood, 'impressionism', sadness. By now, however, it is expected that these features should be complemented by impeccable composition and tight structuring. It is on this very point that misgivings may be expressed. For example, purely in terms of meaning, 'fuite' (l. 1) is an odd word to choose, except it be taken to mean 'fading away' or something similar. And it is ill-chosen if, as has been suggested (Robichez, p. 590), it is a technical term used in painting to mean distance. In that sense its meaning is far from immediate. Admittedly, the appreciation of any poem is determined as much by personal reaction as distinct from the application of various sets of 'artistic' criteria; but in this case there are a number of observable facts (in themselves neither poetic nor unpoetic) to which objections may be raised, if only tentatively. The opening inversion in lines 1–2 is clumsy, 'des' coming too far away from 'fuite'; there is no verb with 'des petits arbres'—a verb is not a necessity, but here its omission reads oddly; and to what noun does 'triste' correspond in verse three? Does it refer to the bird, or to the poet?

The content might be said to be as undistinguished as the composition. There is an evident consistency in the images: 'fuite . . . demi-jour . . . brouiller . . . faible . . . s'efface . . .'. Yet there remain some difficulties in meaning apart from 'fuite'. The most tricky is the word 'lampes' (l. 3). The implication would appear to be that these are *interior* lamps whose light prevents things outside from being clearly seen—though they could be street lamps. As soon as the second verse begins, however, the poem changes from hazy and uncertain outlines to a relatively startling clarity. Verlaine attempts some rather bold juxta-positions in 'l'or—humbles abîmes' and 'doucement s'ensanglante' but only manages to produce an image which is trite in the extreme. He then switches rapidly back to 'humbler' details—a row of trees each with its own sad little bird (?). The reason for the jump is not apparent. The two stanzas sit uneasily together: the one vague, the other com-monplace. The final stanza is an example of the verlainian dying fall (not a good one) as the poet seeks to obliterate all images and all feeling except the vaguest of pleasant melancholy.

In the poem's defence it could be maintained that the lack of cohesion, the general sense of an aimless drifting from one impression to another is all part of the mind's half-awareness of its surroundings (verse one) and of its ultimate lack of interest. On every level, lack of logic is explained by lack of response. What response there is has been reduced to a nebulous feeling of sadness, as usual without cause and without meaning.

The poem is indeed vague. In this case, though, the poet fails to convince because (*a*) he goes too far in sacrificing the structural coherence of the poem; (*b*) he also goes too far in sacrificing the emotional coherence of the poem (verse two) and (*c*) he produces a hotch-potch of lines reminiscent of bits of his earlier poetry. Admittedly, Verlaine's intentions are not known; but it has to be assumed that the poem has turned out this way because Verlaine wanted it this way. As it stands, the end result would seem to suggest that the poet's calculation was miscalculation.

Simples Fresques ii

Perhaps the most interesting information available about this poem is only distantly related to its interpretation. Borel ('Pléiade', p. 1104) recalls Lepelletier's opinion that people like Royer-Collard 'personnifiaient pour son ami les ennemis de la poésie, les solennels et les pontifes', apparently on account of Royer-Collard's 'accueil glacial' of Vigny 'lors de la visite académique de celui-ci'. Robichez puts forward the view that 'sous son apparence gracieuse, ce poème est donc celui de la parodie et du ricanement antisocial' (p. 590), but this depends entirely on seeing the poem in the light of the relationship between Verlaine and Rimbaud and of their assumed attitude to the 'messieurs bien mis' (the interpretation may be valid; one simply does not know). The trouble with the poem is that its significance does seem to lie in its supposed autobiographical explanation. Without it the poem is pleasant—with a touch of irony (?) in:

> J'estimerais beau
> D'être ces vieillards.

The poem exhibits a high regard for symmetry. Each verse follows a pattern of statement plus comment. The sequence of events is straightforward and readily visualised. Indeed, the poem conceals nothing (unless doubts are expressed about 'notre amour'—Rimbaud's . . . or Mathilde's?). Its greatest charm is its wishful thinking.

Chevaux de Bois

The epigraph comes from the second stanza of 'Le Pas d'armes du roi Jean', one of Hugo's *Ballades* (pp. 528–35 in *Œuvres poétiques* vol. i (avant l'exil) 1802–1851, Gallimard, 'Pléiade', édition établie et annotée par Pierre Albouy, 1964). Hugo did not write this particular poem until June 1828. It appeared in the fifth edition in August of the same year. The first edition of what is known now as *Odes et Ballades* was much shorter and was published in June 1822 as *Odes et poésies diverses*.

The poem, a simple tale of soldier and maid enjoying a brief and illicit adventure, is openly anecdotal. Its chief quality is its thinly disguised sexuality, coloured by the poet's slightly ironic treatment of the lovers. What makes the story attractive is not so much its basic appeal to basic instincts as its setting up of two complementary patterns: the 'linear' tale and the 'circular' rhythm, though it is the latter which predominates to the extent of almost totally absorbing the former and not allowing it to go its separate way (as it were) until the last verse. Having established the circular movement in the first verse—and no movement could ever have been more firmly fixed—the poet introduces his story in a way which, while clearly showing its separateness, manages to stress those qualities which tie it best to the circular movement of the fairground roundabout. Apart from the obvious fact that the lovers are actually sitting astride the horses (both of them on one horse? . . . in spite of the plural?), what receives emphasis is the characters' own roundness: 'gros soldat . . . plus grosse bonne'. The horses' circular movement is explicitly mentioned in alternate verses, but the imagery of the intervening verses also carries echoes of the idea of circles: verse four has 'cirque' and, because the hero and heroine are fat, 'ventre'; verse six has 'pigeon et colombe', an acceptable (and natural) extension of the image of rotundity. Even most of the verses which are more or less completely taken over by the repetition of 'tournez' carry extra suggestions of roundness: 'œil . . . piston . . . tambours'.

Do the horses not only possess a horizontal movement but also a vertical one? If so, their up and down motion (overtly sexual) has its own accompanying imagery in the 'piston vainqueur' and the sound (or rather the action) of the drums being beaten.

One further element gives the poem its flavour (already mentioned)—the detached manner in which the poet contemplates the lovers. Neither is attractive. Their situation, for all its excitement, is cheap and tawdry; their surroundings are noisy and vulgar. The poet's attitude is shown well enough in the rather unflattering term 'pigeon'. However, he does give the lovers a romantic exit,

> . . . le ciel en velours
> D'astres en or se vêt lentement

but its sincerity can surely be queried. It recalls (possibly unintentionally) similar conclusions to poems in *La Bonne Chanson*, especially vi, (ll. 13–18):

> Un vaste et tendre
> Apaisement
> Semble descendre
> Du firmament
> Que l'astre irise . . .
> C'est l'heure exquise;

and xix, (ll. 9–12):

> Et quand le soir viendra, l'air sera doux
> Qui se jouera, caressant, dans vos voiles,
> Et les regards paisibles des étoiles
> Bienveillamment souriront aux époux.

The contrast in *tone* could not be clearer.

What 'Chevaux de Bois' achieves is the mechanisation of sentiment. The outcome of the clandestine encounter is not for one second in doubt; it follows as automatically as the horses travel their unending circuit. Just as automatic is the romantic finale—an empty response to a stock situation. Under the gaiety (which must not be reduced let alone dismissed, the poem depends a lot on the excitement it generates) there is a somewhat disenchanted look at the most common of human feelings.

Malines

A poem of limpid speculation, rather unreal, 'Malines' offers a mood untroubled by irony, by questions or by uncertainty. Those few elements which might conceivably have been allowed to ruffle the surface calm are never given the opportunity: the wind's game is harmless, the train makes no sound whatsoever and even the beasts are asleep or peacefully resting. Yet there is something unsatisfactory about the mood. It lacks substance; its tranquillity has no depth. Its visual components have no more reality than the props on a stage. One drifts through it unmoved. Perhaps its point is its very pointlessness.

Why should Fénelon be mentioned? Zayed (p. 24) says that the reference is to a description of the isle of Calypso in *Télémaque*, 'un horizon fait à souhait pour le plaisir des yeux'. Robichez (p. 591) explains the reference thus: 'puisqu'il ne s'agit plus de peindre, mais de se peindre, il est tout naturel qu'apparaissent les souvenirs de lecture'. The reason for this particular memory, rhyme apart, may be a simple association of ideas. The passive contemplation of the peaceful country-side might well have stirred memories of the Fénelon of Quietist persuasion with the emphasis on the subordination of the will and the complete abandonment of the personality to the divine presence . . . but that is pure conjecture. Alternatively, Fénelon may have been associated with sweetness and reasonableness of temperament. Whatever the specific reason, Fénelon seems to have been one of Verlaine's preferred authors and was read while Verlaine was in prison in Belgium (see *Mes Prisons*, 'Prose', p. 346 and p. 351).

BIRDS IN THE NIGHT

The opinions about this short sequence of seven *douzains* vary rather a lot. In the first Pléiade edition of Verlaine's poetry Le Dantec is fulsome in his praise: 'un des plus beaux et des plus déchirants poèmes que Verlaine ait écrits' (p. 931). In the revised edition, Borel (pp. 186–7) expresses substantial reservations, based principally on the poem's obvious autobiographical elements: 'Verlaine pourtant ne peut se dégager longtemps de l'écume la plus superficielle du moi . . . le goût de l'anecdote sentimentale, du fait divers personnel est trop ancré dans sa nature pour ne pas faire intrusion jusque dans les *Romances sans paroles*'. Antoine Adam hesitates before bestowing his approval: '[il y a] une volonté de frôler la prose, de parler tout bas, sur le ton le plus uni et le plus simple. On pourrait goûter mal ces qualités. On pourrait aussi éprouver quelque gêne devant cette illusoire pureté. Mais l'intérêt, la très grande beauté des "Birds in the Night" sont dans la musique de ces vers . . . poésie dégagée de toute rhétorique, toute diaphane, pure spiri-tualité. Pleine de périls à coup sûr, qu'il n'est pas impossible de discerner déjà. Mais pour le moment la réussite est miraculeuse' (p. 99). Zimmermann is noticeably more restrained in her assessment of these poems. Having stated that *Romances sans paroles* is 'un volume étonnant. Comme dans les *Fêtes galantes* il n'y a presque pas de déchets', she adds the following rider in a footnote: ' "Birds in the Night" est la seule partie vraiment contestable' (p. 62). Robichez (p. 591) is categorical about the quality of these verses: 'Birds in the Night' 'nous paraît . . . la partie la moins bien venue des *Romances sans paroles*'. He calls into question both the technical achievement and the emotional climate of the poem; the latter he condemns as 'trop souvent affecté ou odieux'.

The title could have been taken from a song of Arthur Sullivan's popular at the time. On the other hand, it is possible that Verlaine may have intended calling the section the 'Mauvaise Chanson', but the point cannot be proved beyond doubt. The letter to Blémont of 5 October 1872 mentions 'une dizaine de petits poèmes [qui] pourraient en effet se dénommer: "Mauvaise Chanson" '. But Verlaine mentions no specific poems. By December of the same year, Verlaine can write to Blémont—though again without making a specific reference to 'Birds in the Night'—that his volume will contain 'une partie quelque peu élégiaque, mais, je crois, pas glaireuse [an indication of his own doubts about the quality of the poetry?]: quelque chose comme la *Bonne Chanson* retournée, mais combien tendrement! tout caresses et *doux* reproches— en dépit des choses qui sont, je le répète, littéralement hideuses'. At approximately the same date—neither letter carries a precise date— Verlaine writes to Lepelletier that his volume is ready and that its fourth section (to become the third section after the deletion of the 'Nuit Falote'), 'Birds in the Night', will have an epigraph, ironically signed INCONNU, drawn from the third poem of *La Bonne Chanson*:

> En robe grise et verte avec des ruches,
> Un jour de juin que j'étais soucieux,
> Elle apparut souriante à mes yeux
> Qui l'admiraient sans redouter d'embûches.

To the first edition was added a second epigraph from Laclos's *Liaisons dangereuses* (letter 92), 'Elle est si jeune!' Both epigraphs were evidently intended to underline the autobiographical elements in the poem, the second in particular, which, in the novel, continues: 'et sa mère la traite avec tant de sévérité'. (That was not literally the case; perhaps the lines from 'Birds in the Night':

> . . . et la fille aînee
> Etait reparue avec la toilette

are meant as an indication of Mathilde's closeness to and dependence on her mother.) The epigraphs were omitted from later editions.

Verlaine had originally had it in mind to finish the poem after six *douzains*. The seventh appears to have been added at a later date. Zimmermann's opinion (see pp. 244-6) is that the final *douzain* is not closely related to the other six and that its inspiration is more likely to have been Rimbaud than Mathilde. It does indeed seem out of context. The best that can be said for it is that it is a mis-judged climax, mis-judged because it is so perfunctorily prepared (if prepared at all). The rest of the poem concentrates on the relationship between the poet and the woman. The seventh *douzain* concentrates solely on the poet—in itself not unacceptable but which, if it is intended as a conclusion to the previous six verses, is grossly inflated in the sort of sentiment it expresses. Nothing has prepared the reader for such an extreme show of suffering. It can only be concluded that Verlaine's artistic taste was over-ruled by the immediacy of his actual situation and that his sole purpose in writing it was to exonerate himself. In fact, self-exoneration is the one trait which colours the whole set of *douzains*. The trait is not necessarily illegitimate poetically speaking; it is a question of how that particular feeling is put across—and the poem as a whole raises doubts about the manner in which the sentiment is conveyed. Verlaine's hope that the section he describes as 'quelque peu élégiaque' should not be too 'glaireuse' is perhaps a pointer in the right direction. He was evidently aware that the poem displayed a tendency towards maw-kishness. And it certainly does: the poet excuses himself from any blame; he is

> un bon soldat
> Blessé

(a neat touch, given Verlaine's active distaste for soldierly duties!); he bleeds, he suffers; his martyrdom is exquisitely painful yet he can find it in him to be full of forgiveness for the woman's shortcomings; he finds it difficult—because of the pain—to mention her treachery and lack of understanding (but he does, with masochistic enjoyment) . . . and so it goes on. The poet's raw self-pity and self-righteousness are doubtless *material* for poetry. They are out of place *as poetry*. Feelings so blatantly self-centred become a source of literary embarrassment and are ultimately unwelcome. The sincerity of Verlaine's real feelings, no matter how much his suffering may be thought to be unjustified, is not in question. What is at stake is the attempt—or so it seems—to transfer the feelings intact on to the page. Verlaine succeeds in versifying the feelings without achieving much that could be called poetry. All this is admittedly no more than supposition, but it arises out of a sense of discomfort which no amount of sympathetic reading can dispel. Ver-laine's characteristic simplicity of presentation—in the 'Ariettes oubliées' a source of great subtlety—serves only to underline the crudeness of much of 'Birds in the Night'.

There is one unexplained technical point: the rhyme scheme is *a b a b* throughout except for the fourth verse which is *a b b a*. Is it carelessness, or is it deliberate? Had Verlaine wished he could have continued to use the normal rhyme scheme by inverting the first two lines and changing a little of the punctuation:

> Quand je vous disais, dans mes moments noirs,
> —Et vous voyez bien que j'avais raison—
> Que vos yeux, foyer de mes vieux espoirs,
> Ne couvaient plus rien que la trahison,
> Vous juriez alors . . .

Heresy, no doubt. The point seems hardly worth making. In a poem of such ill-concealed insincerity and such belligerent innocence the tech-nical achievements can never be more than of secondary importance.

AQUARELLES

Green

The meaning of the title is unclear. It could come from an obvious association with the greenery of the first line . . . it could equally be held to refer to the poem's aura of innocence and inexperience. Neither Verlaine's correspondence nor his prose works produces any clue. In fact, the poem receives no mention at all in Verlaine's letters so that even the date of its composition is unknown. Borel ('Pléiade', p. 187), following the argument of Saffrey and Bouillane de Lacoste (see the *Mercure de France* August 1956), suggests that the poem was written some time between October and December 1872. The suggestion is quite plausible. The first time Verlaine mentions the section as a whole is in the letter to Blémont dated 22 April 1873: 'Je vous envoie ci-joint deux petites pièces destinées aux *Romances sans paroles*. Je les extrais d'une partie anglaise intitulée "Aquarelles" '. The two poems are 'A Poor Young Shepherd' and 'Child Wife' (written as 'The Child Wife'), the latter (only?) dated 2 April 1873.

The rolling sonority of these lines, the relative purity of sentiment (or so it appears), are exceptional in *Romances sans paroles*. On other counts too the poem is exceptional; the syntactical simplicity covers no representational vagueness, and the clarity of the imagery finds a substantial echo in the classical correctness of the rhythm. In these respects the poem would not appear out of place in *La Bonne Chanson*. In its position in the collection, the contrast with both 'Birds in the Night' and 'Child Wife' is startling. Explanations which have recourse to the brief reunion of Verlaine and Mathilde in Brussels are rather too precise for a poem the main effect of which is the creation of an aura of sensual pleasure.

The poem begins by giving the impression that it could be a verbal transposition of, say, a typical Victorian romantic painting with the young man on his knees bearing gifts to a suitably demure young lady. The setting is idyllic, the situation idealized. But the poem follows an odd line of development. In it there is what must be a considerable hiatus. In fact, the poem leaves unsaid the part of the story in which the young man's desire is actually consummated. Stanza three must assume a longish interval between itself and stanza two. This latter ends on a note of anticipation. The 'chers instants', however, are passed over in decent silence—yet something has happened by the time stanza three opens. The young man was originally at the feet of the girl, a proper place from which to offer his (rather large?) bouquet. In any case, being on his knees is restful since he confesses to feeling tired. Stanza three finds him in a less decorous position. Had the transition from stanza two been accomplished without a break in the time sequence one might have expected the young man's new position to have brought with it a keen sense of anticipation. On the contrary, what is expressed is the evident result of pleasure fulfilled. 'La bonne tempête' has blown itself out. Nor is the young man the only one so affected. The demure young lady has, as it were, not been inactive because stanza three shows her 'resting' having bestowed her 'derniers baisers'. The opening image of an entirely chaste relationship has disappeared and yet the poem manages to retain an air of purity. It does so because there are no recriminations and no ironic comments. All is joy and satisfaction.

Spleen

'... le poème est profondément mystérieux. Ses symboles sont encore plus difficiles à interpréter parce qu'ils sont entièrement personnels, liés sans doute à cet univers affectif et spirituel dont Verlaine veut nous cacher l'existence. Le poème se compose d'images hermétiques qui ont été juxtaposées selon le mode d'expression favori de Rimbaud' (Zimmermann, p. 247). Much depends on whether or not the individual images in the poem are seen as unexplained keys to specific events, places or people, over which Verlaine is drawing an impenetrable veil. But specific interpretations are not necessary. The poem's impact is not lessened because one is not sure if the poem is addressed to Rimbaud or Mathilde. Adam (p. 100) thinks that it relates to Mathilde, ' "Spleen", c'est la nostalgie du paradis perdu en un cœur las de toutes choses, mais non pas, hélas! de Mathilde'. Robichez (p. 594), basing his reasoning on line eight—'Quelque fuite atroce de vous'—prefers to think that Verlaine 'transpose au féminin les sentiments que lui inspire Rimbaud'. To attribute the poem's meaning to one or to the other (both are plausible) is scarcely to make more sense of it as it stands on the page. What is important is the feeling the poem articulates, not the situation from which the feeling is supposed, rightly or wrongly, to have come. The poet's refusal either to name or to indicate a place—the various objects named, 'roses', 'ciel', 'lierres' and so on, hardly constitute more than a rudimentary setting of an anonymous sort—should be sufficient in itself to suggest that specific sources or incidents are irrelevant to the poem's meaning (though not necessarily to its generation). 'Spleen' is what the poem expresses in a series of statements designed to illustrate, if that is the word, the title. The objects named are qualified in such a way as to produce a slight feeling of unease. They become a shade unreal; they can no longer be sympathetic. In fact the poet seems to prefer their muted hostility. Solace cannot be found in the poet's companion either, though his companion is at the same time the source of the poet's happiness. What disturbs him is his sense of the impermanence of the relationship. This, coupled with his complete emotional attachment to the relationship, gives rise to a feeling of such distressing insecurity that the smallest incident,

> Chère, pour peu que tu te bouges,
> Renaissent tous mes désespoirs,

is intensified beyond all reason and occasions a reaction which is exaggerated out of all proportion. The possibility of the companion leaving is immediately built into 'quelque fuite atroce'. The poet's spleen is a state of hypersensitivity and depression. He lives on the raw edges of his nerves yet, capable of recognising his plight, he is incapable of doing anything to change it. He is both willing and unwilling victim of his own feelings: 'Je suis las . . . de tout, fors de vous, hélas!' The poem affords no relief and no possibility of relief.

The poem's structure is without complications: a descriptive verse alternates with a verse relating to the poet's reaction (verses five and six vary the pattern to some extent). Within the larger pattern smaller patterns are discernible (taking for granted the repetitive use of individual words and sounds), especially within the first four verses. The descriptive verses are totally static (Verlaine uses 'être') and are in the past. The verses containing the poet's reactions imply movement and are in the present. Verses one and three have a neat arrangement of noun, verb and adjectives; verses two and four combine the poet and the companion. Stanzas five and six, not as sharply divided from each other, act as a summing up. As in most of Verlaine's best poetry, no matter how intense the feelings expressed, the poet remains in complete technical control. It is his control which, by containing and compressing the sentiment, allows the poem to build up successfully its affective tension.

Streets i

Some doubt has been cast on Thomas Gringoire's account in the *Courrier de Londres*, 2 December 1911, of the place where this poem was written. Gringoire's version is as follows: 'Un jour qu'il avait bien voulu, avec quelle ardeur singulière, nous dire *la Gigue*, Verlaine me raconta qu'il avait écrit ces vers dans un bar qui se trouve à l'angle de Old Compton Street et de Greek Street'. But, as Underwood rightly points out, (*Verlaine et l'Angleterre*, p. 108) as early as September 1872 Verlaine had been struck by a peculiar habit some Londoners had of dancing the jig in public. He wrote to Lepelletier in the same month: 'dans les cafés-concerts, Alhambra, Grecian Theater . . . on danse la gigue entre deux *God save* . . .'.

The use of a light-hearted refrain, promising good humour and frivolity, is a little deceptive. As it turns out, the simple exhortation: 'Dansons la gigue!' is a source of considerable variation, taking as it does its emotional flavour from the verse which precedes it. To begin with it is no more than a straightforward invitation. The poet's story, however, has already taken place; the poet used to love a young girl distinguished, as they all are, by her eyes which are not only 'jolis' and 'clairs' but also 'malicieux'. Therein lies the moral of the tale. Such a characteristic, no matter how attractive, should have warned the poet that it was dangerous to become emotionally involved. Yet the eyes were evidently irresistible. The poet fell for them. And he suffered accordingly, though not without getting a certain amount of pleasure from the adventure. On its third appearance: 'Dansons la gigue!' suggests both regret and relief. Then the story takes a new turn. What had at first been fairly pleasant 'suffering' changes to the enjoyment of the physical side of the relationship for its own sake. The poet has now passed out of the stage of emotional involvement to one of indifference—though the relationship has not yet come to an end. His enjoyment is that of the libertine. 'Dansons la gigue!' only serves to highlight the mechanical nature of the exercise. But the poet, being a poet, cannot simply tuck his heart away in his back pocket; he much prefers to wear it on his sleeve. With an alacrity that betrays a fondness for the occasional wallow in melancholic nostalgia, he recalls his past *amour* with a nicely calculated touch of lachrymose regret. 'Dansons la gigue!' has now taken on an air of forced gaiety. The poet puts on a brave face—or pretends to. The poem, after all, is only lightweight. It might be a mistake to read too much personal tragedy into it.

Is Verlaine's use of a three line stanza a conscious imitation of the triple time of the jig proper? Or is it simply coincidence? There is one more technical point worth noting: Verlaine had long been aware of the advantage to be gained by simple repetition—see his article on Baudelaire ('Prose', p. 611) where, admittedly for reasons connected with certain qualities in Baudelaire's poetry, he writes of repetition the aim of which is to keep bringing back the same line 'autour d'une idée toujours nouvelle et réciproquement'. 'Streets' admirably proves its effectiveness.

Streets ii

Writing from prison at Mons, 24 November 1873, Verlaine instructs Lepelletier: 's'il en est temps encore, dans la pièce: *O la rivière dans la rue!* mettre au 4e vers [a mistake, he meant the third]: *Derrière un mur haut de cinq pieds*, au lieu de—*entre 2 murs* . . . Je me souviens qu'il n'y a, en effet, qu'un mur, l'autre côté étant au niveau du *ground*'. It was not until the second edition, however, that the alteration was made.

'Streets ii' is almost pure description—the actual site the poem describes has been located (see Underwood, p. 104). Of all the poems in *Romances sans paroles* this is one of the most easily understood once the opening three lines have been seen in the context of the poem as a whole. Verlaine does no more than tinge the poem with a vague aura of sadness. It is unlikely that the emotional atmosphere, such as it is, is meant as an extension of the poet's mood though doubtless the appearance of the river (canal) is conducive to ill-defined but rather sombre reflections. To that extent the poem goes beyond description for its own sake; but it does not go very far.

The most notable feature of the poem lies in the treatment of the octosyllabic line. By omitting punctuation at the end of more than half the lines (in particular ll. 4–6 and 7–10) Verlaine succeeds in giving the lines a stateliness which they would not, as pure rhythm, possess. Obviously the lines are read according to the meaning of the words (and the dominant words are the verbs 'roule' and 'dévale ample'); none the less there is the semblance of a concordance of sound and sense which, within the limits of such a short poem, is impressive.

The poem may have been intended as one of a projected series of *croquis londoniens*. It is as 'English' as anything else Verlaine wrote, but its Englishness derives from the use of one word—'cottages'—and from the incidental knowledge that it was written about an identifiable place in London.

Child Wife

The title is apparently borrowed from Dickens's *David Copperfield* where it is applied to Dora. At one point Verlaine changed his mind about the title and substituted 'The Pretty One'. It was never used in subsequent editions. Underwood thinks it may have been suggested by the opening lines of a contemporary song:

> My little pretty one,
> My pretty bonny one,
> She is a joyous one,
> And gentle as can be . . .

If that is so, it serves only to underline the rather cruelly ironic nature of the substitution, since the girl depicted in the poem is singularly unattractive.

Written in the same vein as 'Birds in the Night', 'Child Wife' exhibits the identical frantic denial of faults, the same flagrant off-loading of responsibility and the same wearisome assertion that the poet combines in his own misunderstood person all the desirable qualities a perfect husband should have. Had it ever been given the title 'Mauvaise

Chanson' it would have been better served. Is it at all a commentary on the quality of this poem and of 'Birds in the Night' that Verlaine, in the *Choix de poésies* of 1891, Charpentier, included all the *Romances sans paroles* except for these two?

A Poor Young Shepherd

Various sources of inspiration are put forward for this poem (see in particular Underwood, pp. 106–7). Among the most likely are, firstly, Shakespeare's *Hamlet* where Ophelia has the lines:

> Tomorrow is Saint Valentine's day,
> All in the morning betime,
> And I a maid at your window,
> To be your Valentine;

Ophelia, let it be noted, is taking leave of her senses; and secondly an obscure Valentine published in the *Gentleman's Magazine*, 14 February 1873, wherein it is advocated that a young man should send his sweetheart a kiss on St Valentine's day. Zayed (p. 342) has traced possible influences from such sources as Hugo, Leconte de Lisle and, more especially, Marceline Desbordes-Valmore. In the last mentioned it is the supposed: 'volonté d'unir la simplicité de la forme à celle du fond' which this poem, along with others, is said to illustrate. In this instance it is the young man who is afraid of being kissed (and the association of the kiss with a bee-sting gives the young man in question a curious sexual ambiguity) even though he professes to love the girl. In the light of his reluctance to kiss her it is unexpected to find him complaining of the difficulty of being a lover. Perhaps the difficulty lies in his having to restrain his ardour . . . the 'Vieilles Bonnes Chansons' are evidence enough of what kissing is about! . . . in the sure knowledge, 'fort heureusement', that the girl will be totally available in due course.

In a poem which cannot really be said to be much more than pleasantly inconsequential Verlaine still manages to hint at a suppressed sexuality, the nature of which he leaves somewhat undecided.

Structurally the poem is neat. The overall stanza pattern, 1 2 3 4 1, is echoed in the construction of the individual verses though the final line of verses 2, 3 and 4 is not an exact copy of the first line. To carry the pattern even further, the five verses of five lines are written in lines of five syllables. Verlaine would seem to be enjoying a certain amount of self-indulgent word-play (or number-play).

Beams

Assuming that Verlaine is accurate in his dating of this poem, then it was written on board the ship taking him from Dover to Ostend on 4 April 1873. And unless one has an innate mistrust of the poet there is no reason to doubt his word on this point. But that is where the clarity stops. Although the poem seems straightforward it offers problems of interpretation which, to date, have not been entirely satisfactorily solved. To begin with, its title is not intelligible. 'Beams' refers, perhaps, to the sun's rays and their effect on the girl's blonde hair. Further than that it would be unwise to go, especially in the light of Verlaine's peculiar command of English at this date. As for an interpretation of the poem as a whole, a variety of suggestions have been put forward: 'elle' is Rimbaud in disguise; 'elle' is a passenger on the boat 'confondue avec le navire, selon un mouvement tout baudelairien'; she seems to walk on the water drawing after her all the other passengers 'dans une traversée fantastique' (see Robichez, p. 596). Going beyond this, Bornecque (p. 92) writes of 'le miracle d'une femme ou d'une jeune fille, anonyme et radieuse, qui abandonne le pont du bateau pour marcher sur la mer, tandis que la suivent sans peine ni surprise tous ceux qui ont foi en elle . . . *Passage tout uni du naturel au surnaturel*'; and Borel ('Poésie', p. 149) talks of 'la surréalité émerveillée de ce poème [qui] transfigure le souvenir d'une traversée qui fut, suivant Verlaine "inouï de beauté" '. More recently D. D. R. Owen (in *French Studies*, April 1971, pp. 156–61), relying on what he thinks was Verlaine's knowledge of the Bible and on his certain interest in the English habit of open-air preaching and hymn singing, finds in 'elle' a surrogate for Christ and at the same time a 'defiant hymn for the Epoux infernal . . . a supreme and almost mystical tribute' to Rimbaud. It is almost impossible to arrive at any one, definite, interpretation. Verlaine on the other hand does happen to mention the poem in his correspondence. The letter of 23 May 1873 has this to say: 'les petites pièces: "Le piano" etc.; "Oh triste, triste" etc.; J'ai peur d'un baiser . . . ; Beams . . . et autres, témoignent, au besoin, assez en faveur de ma parfaite amour pour le "sesque" . . .'. He is, of course, forestalling possible accusations of homosexuality (in the poetry . . . and in his life?). If his choice of poems is carefully thought out then 'Beams' is about a young unnamed *woman* on the ship whom Verlaine and his companion follow around the deck in a game of mild flirtation. An incident such as that could well have given rise to the poem. The point is, does the poem transcend the anecdote sufficiently in order to operate at quite another level (whatever that level may be) or is the anecdote simply embroidered with snatches of mystery and hints of deeper meaning (which do not lead anywhere)? Whatever the case—and one is free to make one's choice—the poem is a serene enough ending to the collection, a return to a traditional way of writing with all its plenitude and assurance.

(For a different and necessarily curtailed set of commentaries see Chadwick, pp. 35–51.)

NOTES

INTRODUCTION

1. Anatole France was never capable of producing a detached assessment of Verlaine's poetry. His impressions of the man always managed to cloud his literary judgement. See the pages on Verlaine in France's *La Vie littéraire*, troisième série; Calmann-Lévy, 1925, pp. 309–18.

2. For a thorough examination of Verlaine's probable state of mind prior to the publication of *La Bonne Chanson* see J.-S. Chaussivert, *L'Art verlainien dans 'La Bonne Chanson'*, Nizet, 1973. Chaussivert is one of the few contemporary critics who thinks quite highly of this volume of neglected or much despised poems.

3. Eléonore Zimmermann devotes a whole chapter of *Magies de Verlaine* to examining the possible shape his 'système' might have taken (see pp. 89–123). Her suggestions are interesting but not conclusive.

4. The most convenient book in which to consult Morice's article and Verlaine's letter of reply is *Paul Verlaine. Lettres inédites à Charles Morice*, publiées et annotées par Georges Zayed, Droz-Minard, 1964. The article is quoted in full in the Introduction pp. li–lii; Verlaine's letter is on pp. 3–4.

5. The list could be extended legitimately to include the names of poets of Verlaine's own generation—Mendès, Mérat, Glatigny and so on.

6. It may be worth pointing out that Verlaine, for much of the period of composition of *Romances sans paroles*, was without his own books and depended upon libraries for his reading. He may not have read much French poetry . . . ?

Verlaine's technique in parts of *Romances sans paroles* has been likened to that of the Impressionists. Although the idea is productive of interesting parallels, there cannot have been much occasion for direct influence (simply from a historical point of view). Verlaine had evidently met such artists as Degas, Monet, Manet, Forain and Renoir, and on at least four separate occasions he mentions Fantin-Latour's painting 'Coin de table' in which he himself is portrayed. That is the limit of his recorded concern. It may well have been true that Verlaine was a party to discussions on the then new technique of 'impressionism' (not given that name in any case until 1874) but the effect, if any, on his poetry is impossible to determine. What is at stake is the question of similarities, much more so than the possibility of literal borrowing. Nadal offers a lucid exposé of the idea based on the suggestion that just as the painters 'se sont livrés passionnément à la sensation pour elle-même', so Verlaine 's'était tourné résolument vers un art dont la sensation constituait la base' (pp. 96–9). The comparison is illuminating, but it works at the level of instinctive juxtapositioning and not at the level of genuine technical comparison. Borel ('Pléiade', pp. 182–5) develops the parallel in even greater detail: 'notes brèves juxtaposées, touches de couleur ou de lumière, ce sont là les vrais éléments constitutifs du poème, comme, sur la toile où Monet ou Pissarro les dispose, c'est le bleu et non la robe ou le ciel, le rouge et non le toit, l'ocre et non le mur qui constituent le tableau', but in spite of all that, he has to concede that 'la poésie de Verlaine n'est aucunement une transposition dans l'ordre du langage de l'art des peintres impressionnistes'. What may have started off the whole idea in the first place was Verlaine's remark in the letter of 5 October 1872 to Blémont that *Romances sans paroles* was 'une série d'impressions vagues, tristes et gaies . . .'. Perhaps the idea could be left at that appropriate level of vagueness.

7. If one is interested in detailed analyses of the sound content of Verlaine's poetry, there exist two close studies of 'Il pleure dans mon cœur': by Guy Michaud in *Connaissance de la littérature* and by Paul Delbouille in *Poésie et sonorités*.

COMPOSITION/PUBLICATION OF 'ROMANCES SANS PAROLES'

1872   *18 May:* 'Ariette oubliée'i, 'C'est l'extase langoureuse', published
        in the *Renaissance littéraire et artistique.*
        29 June: 'Ariette oubliée' v, 'Le piano que baise une main frêle',
        published in the same periodical.
        The remaining *ariettes* all written by the end of June.[1]
        July–August—'Paysages Belges' written.[2]
        September–October—'Birds in the Night' written.[3]
1873   By the end of *February* the 'Aquarelles' partially completed:
        'Green', 'Spleen', 'Streets i and ii' written(?)
        2 April 'Child Wife' and 'A poor young shepherd' written.[4]
        4 April 'Beams'.
1874   *March: Romances sans paroles* published.

1. Assuming Verlaine's indication, 'Mai–juin 1872', is taken to refer
to the complete sequence of 'Ariettes oubliées'. The point is not estab-
lished beyond all doubt.

2. Assuming Verlaine's dating is correct. There seems to be no reason
for questioning it.

3. See Introduction pp. 10–11 and Verlaine's own dating.

4. Again, Verlaine's own dating.

As far as can be ascertained *Romances sans paroles* is arranged
chronologically—at least with regard to the four main sections.

SELECT BIBLIOGRAPHY

Exceptionally a book receives its full bibliographical details in the text
or the notes in those few cases where its relative lack of importance
regarding Verlaine does not call for its inclusion in the following list.

EDITIONS

Paul Verlaine, *Œuvres complètes* (2 vols.), introduction d'Octave Nadal,
études et notes de Jacques Borel, Le Club du meilleur livre, 1959–60.
(All quotations from Verlaine's correspondence are taken from vol. i,
pp. 952–1076.)

Paul Verlaine, *Œuvres poétiques complètes*, texte établi et annoté par Y.-G.
Le Dantec, édition révisée par Jacques Borel, Gallimard, Bibliothèque
de la Pléiade, 1962 (cited as 'Pléiade').

Paul Verlaine, *Œuvres poétiques*, édition de Jacques Robichez, Garnier,
1969.

Paul Verlaine, *Fêtes galantes, Romances sans paroles* précédé de *Poèmes
Saturniens*, préface et notes de Jacques Borel, Gallimard, 'Poésie', 1973.

Paul Verlaine, *Fêtes galantes, La Bonne Chanson, Romances sans paroles*, avec
introduction et notes de V. P. Underwood, Editions de l'Université de
Manchester, nouvelle éd. revue et corrigée, 1963.

Verlaine, *Selected Poems*, edited by R. C. D. Perman, Oxford University
Press, 1965.

Paul Verlaine, *Œuvres en prose complètes*, texte établi, présenté et annoté
par Jacques Borel, Gallimard, Bibliothèque de la Pléiade, 1972 (cited
as 'Prose').

CRITICISM

Antoine Adam, *Verlaine*, nouvelle éd. Hatier, 'Connaissance des lettres',
1961.

J.-H. Bornecque, *Verlaine par lui-même*, Editions du Seuil, 1966.

A. E. Carter, *Verlaine, a Study in Parallels*, University of Toronto Press,
1969.

C. Chadwick, *Verlaine*, 'Athlone French Poets', The Athlone Press,
1973.

Paul Delbouille, *Poésie et sonorités. La critique contemporaine devant le pouvoir
suggestif des sons*, Les Belles Lettres, 1961.

E. Lepelletier, *Paul Verlaine, sa vie, son œuvre*, Mercure de France, 1907.

Guy Michaud, *Connaissance de la littérature. L'œuvre et ses techniques*, Nizet, 1957.

Charles Morice, *Paul Verlaine*, Vanier, 1888.

Charles Morice, *La Littérature de tout à l'heure*, Perrin, 1889.

Octave Nadal, *Paul Verlaine*, Mercure de France, 1961.

François Porché, *Verlaine tel qu'il fut*, Flammarion, 1933.

J.-P. Richard, *Poésie et Profondeur*, Editions du Seuil, 1955.

Joanna Richardson, *Verlaine*, Weidenfeld and Nicolson, 1971.

A. Saffrey and H. de Bouillane de Lacoste, 'Verlaine et les *Romances sans paroles*', *Mercure de France*, 1 August 1956.

V. P. Underwood, *Verlaine et l'Angleterre*, Nizet, 1956.

ex-Madame Paul Verlaine, *Mémoires de ma vie*, Flammarion, 1935.

Georges Zayed, *La Formation littéraire de Verlaine*, nouvelle éd. augmentée, Nizet, 1970.

Eléonore M. Zimmermann, *Magies de Verlaine*, Corti, 1967.

DATE DUE